Drawing Out Learning With Thinking Maps®

A Guide for Teaching and Assessment in Pre-K–2

Shelly L. Counsell and David Hyerle

Foreword by Yvette Jackson

TEACHERS COLLEGE PRESS

TEACHERS COLLEGE | COLUMBIA UNIVERSITY
NEW YORK AND LONDON

Published by Teachers College Press,® 1234 Amsterdam Avenue, New York, NY 10027

Front cover design by Pete Donahue.

Library of Congress Cataloging-in-Publication Data

Names: Counsell, Shelly L., author. | Hyerle, David, author.
Title: Drawing out learning with Thinking Maps : a guide for teaching and
    assessment in Pre-K–2 / Shelly L. Counsell and David Hyerle.
Description: New York, NY : Teachers College Press, 2023. | Includes bibliographical references
    and index. | Summary: "As a visual language framework, Thinking Maps® offers a way for
    young learners to represent their ideas by visually mapping their fundamental patterns
    of thinking. The authors offer a wide range of materials, strategies, and evidence-based
    practices for implementing with Pre-K–2 children"— Provided by publisher.
Identifiers: LCCN 2022055169 (print) | LCCN 2022055170 (ebook) |
    ISBN 9780807767764 (paperback) | ISBN 9780807767771 (hardcover) |
    ISBN 9780807781432 (ebook)
Subjects: LCSH: Thought and thinking—Study and teaching (Early childhood) |
    Thought and thinking—Study and teaching (Elementary) | Cognition in children. |
    Visual learning.
Classification: LCC LB1590.3 .C687 2023 (print) | LCC LB1590.3 (ebook) |
    DDC 370.15/2—dc23/eng/20230217
LC record available at https://lccn.loc.gov/2022055169
LC ebook record available at https://lccn.loc.gov/2022055170

ISBN 978-0-8077-6776-4 (paper)
ISBN 978-0-8077-6777-1 (hardcover)
ISBN 978-0-8077-8143-2 (ebook)

Printed on acid-free paper
Manufactured in the United States of America

Dedication

Dr. Arthur Costa is one of the very few visionary leaders across all education-related fields who, through clarity, persistence, empathy, and thought-filled collaboration, has achieved multigenerational ripple effects in educational outcomes for all learners, as a direct result of his impactful contributions designed to improve the quality of teaching practices around the globe. His insights have inspired us to offer to young minds (and the teachers who work with them) some first steps toward responding to the eternal question he advanced many decades ago, with continued and growing relevance even today: *How* are you thinking?

Contents

List of Figures   vii

List of Tables   xi

Foreword   *Yvette Jackson*   xiii

Acknowledgments   xv

Introduction: Can I Use Thinking Maps With Young Children? Yes, You Can!   1

Thinking Maps: Integrating Three Types of Visual Tools   2

Why Early Childhood?   3

Thinking Maps as a Learning, Teaching, and Assessment Framework   4

1. Bringing Thinking Maps to Life   9

Learning Trajectories and Developmental Progressions   9

The Five Critical Attributes of Thinking Maps   12

TMaps Tap Into Prior Knowledge and Experience   14

Thinking Maps Exemplifies Universally Designed Learning (UDL)   15

Conclusion   21

2. Thinking Maps Across Developmental Domains   22

Developmentally Appropriate Practice   22

Domain 1—Cognitive Development   24

Domain 2—Socioemotional Development   28

Domain 3—Physical and Healthy   29

Domain 4—General Learning Competencies   29

Conclusion   30

3. Thinking Maps Across Academic Content Areas   **31**

Thinking Maps Inspire Talking, Reading, and Writing   32

Thinking Maps Support Logical-Mathematical Reasoning   42

Thinking Maps Promote Scientific Thinking, Reasoning, and Inquiry   44

Engineering Design and Technology With Thinking Maps   54

Social Studies Instruction and Thinking Maps   55

Related Early Childhood Approaches and Curricula   57

Conclusion   59

**4. Thinking Maps Promote Democratic Learning Communities With
     Full Community Membership**   **60**

Thinking Maps Promote Responsive, Democratic Learning   60

Conclusion   71

**5. Thinking Maps Provide Authentic Formative Assessment
     and Documentation**   **72**

A Brief Historical Perspective of Standardized Testing   72

Classroom Assessments   74

Conclusion   80

6. The Science Underlying Thinking Maps With Young Children   **81**

Research and Theoretical Foundation for Thinking Maps   81

Executive Function   81

Self-Regulation   84

Habits of Mind   85

Alignment With Standards   87

Conclusion   89

Appendix: Glossary   **91**

References   **93**

Index   **105**

About the Authors   **111**

List of Figures

Figure I.1	Thinking Maps	2
Figure 1.1	Circle Map: Brainstorming About Mice	10
Figure 1.2	Bubble-Map: Adjectives Describing Mice	10
Figure 1.3	Flow Map: Sequencing a Food Chain Including Mice	11
Figure 1.4	Large Plastic Tablecloth Maps	18
Figure 1.5	Small Individual Vinyl Place Mat Maps	18
Figure 1.6	Colored Plastic Overlays	18
Figure 1.7	Bubble Map: Describing Mice With a Frame of Reference Added	19
Figure 1.8	Multi-Flow Map: Cause–Effect Outcomes of Undigested Nutrients for Animals and Plant Life	20
Figure 2.1	Computer-Generated Circle Map: Brainstorming About Whales and Sharks	26
Figure 2.2	Circle Map: Brainstorming About Sharks	26
Figure 2.3	Circle Map: Brainstorming About Whales	26
Figure 2.4	Computer-Generated Double-Bubble Map: Comparing/Contrasting Sharks and Whales	27
Figure 2.5	Double-Bubble Map: Comparing/Contrasting Sharks and Whales	27
Figure 3.1	Bubble Map: Describing a Mystery Item (Ostrich) in the Feely Bag	32
Figure 3.2	Bubble Map: Additional Adjectives Describing an Ostrich	33
Figure 3.3	T-Chart—Mystery Item Questions and Answers	33
Figure 3.4	Circle Map—Brainstorming About Bears	36
Figure 3.5	Bubble Map—Describing Goldilocks	37
Figure 3.6	Double-Bubble Map—Comparing and Contrasting Goldilocks and Baby Bear	37
Figure 3.7	Flow Map: Sequencing Explored Belongings by Goldilocks	37
Figure 3.8	Brace Map: Part–Whole Relationship to Chairs	37
Figure 3.9	Tree Map: Classifying the Three Bears' Belongings	38
Figure 3.10	Bridge Map: Analogies of How Goldilocks Experienced Each Item	38
Figure 3.11	Multi-Flow Map: Cause–Effect Used to Make Porridge	39
Figure 3.12	Circle Map: Brainstorming Wintertime With a Source Reference Frame	39
Figure 3.13	Bubble Map: Describing a Snowman	40
Figure 3.14	Brace Map: Parts of a Snowman	40
Figure 3.15	Flow Map: Sequencing Snowman Construction	40
Figure 3.16	Bridge Map: Singular and Plural Winter Item Analogies	40

Figure 3.17   Double-Bubble Map: Compare/Contrast *Snowballs* and
                The Snowy Day   41
Figure 3.18   Circle Map: Conceptual Subitizing "6"   42
Figure 3.19   Flow Map: Conceptual Subitizing and Counting "6–10"   42
Figure 3.20   Tree Map: Classifying Geometric Shapes   43
Figure 3.21   Tree Map: Classifying Three-Dimensional Solids by Shape   43
Figure 3.22   Flow Map: Sequencing Adding With Regrouping   44
Figure 3.23   Inquiry Teaching Model (adapted from Counsell et al., 2016)   46
Figure 3.24   Brace Map: Parts of a Tulip in Spanish and English   48
Figure 3.25   Brace Map: Parts of a Tree (Large Group)   48
Figure 3.26   Brace Map: Parts of a Tree (Individual)   49
Figure 3.27   Flow Map: Sequencing Seed Germination   49
Figure 3.28   Flow Map: Sequencing the Apple Tree Life Cycle   49
Figure 3.29   Tree Map: Classifying Living Organisms and Nonliving Items   49
Figure 3.30   Tree Map: Classifying Vertebrates and Invertebrates   50
Figure 3.31   Tree Map: Classifying Animals Born Alive or Hatched
                From Eggs   50
Figure 3.32   Double-Bubble Map: Compare and Contrast Animals
                and Plant Life   50
Figure 3.33   Multi-Flow Map: Extreme Factors Causing Plants to Die   51
Figure 3.34   Tree Map: Classifying Biodegradable and Non-Biodegradable Items   51
Figure 3.35   Bubble Map: Describing the Attributes of a Marble   52
Figure 3.36   Double-Bubble Map: Compare and Contrast Motion Objects   53
Figure 3.37   Tree Map: Classifying Objects by Motion   53
Figure 3.38   Tree Map: Classifying Objects by Motion   53
Figure 3.39   Bridge Map: Analyzing Motion–Object Analogies   54
Figure 3.40   Flow Map: Sequencing a Toy Car Design Process   55
Figure 3.41   Bubble Map: Describing the Office of the President
                (Group Work)   56
Figure 3.42   Bubble Map: Describing the Office of the President
                (Group Work)   56
Figure 3.43   Bubble Map: Describing the Office of the President Completed   56
Figure 4.1   Student Voice—Key Aspects in Relation to TMaps   61
Figure 4.2   Learner Agency: Low Agency vs. High Agency   62
Figure 4.3   Brace Map: Parts of My Favorite Outfit   62
Figure 4.4   Flow Map: Sequencing Tasks to Get Ready for School   62
Figure 4.5   Multi-Flow Map: Cause–Effect With Pumpkins Used to
                Enjoy Halloween   62
Figure 4.6   Cycle of Authentic Student Voice and Agency   64
Figure 4.7   Tree Map: Classifying Rules According to Location   65
Figure 4.8   Circle Map: Brainstorming Breakfast Menu Items   68
Figure 4.9   Circle Map: Brainstorming Breakfast Menu Items   68
Figure 5.1   Circle Map: Brainstorming Different Amounts Equaling
                One Dollar   76
Figure 5.2   Tree Map: Classifying U.S. Coins   76
Figure 5.3   Bridge Map: Coin and Monetary Value Analogy   77
Figure 5.4   Tree Map: Classifying Items by the Five Senses   77
Figure 5.5   Brace Map: Parts of an Apple   77
Figure 5.6   Brace Map: Parts of an Apple   77

Figure 5.7   Graphing Favorite Type of Apple Using Five Senses   78
Figure 5.8   Bridge Map: Body Parts and Five Sense Analogies   78
Figure 5.9   Multi-Flow Map: Cause–Effect Relationship Between
              Sensations and the Brain   78
Figure 5.10   Multi-Flow Map: Cause–Effect Relationship Between
              Sensations and the Brain   78
Figure 5.11   Bubble Map: Using Senses to Describe Apples   79
Figure 5.12   Double-Bubble Map: Comparing and Contrasting Apples   79
Figure 5.13   Bubble Map: Using Senses to Describe Popcorn (Whole Group) 79
Figure 5.14   Bubble Map: Using Senses to Describe Popcorn (Individual) 79
Figure 6.1   Flow Map: Sequencing the Children's Story *All Fall Down* 82
Figure 6.2   Flow Map: Sequencing Clothing Items in *Froggy Gets Dressed* 83
Figure 6.3   Flow Maps: Sequencing the Butterfly Life Cycle   83
Figure 6.4   Double-Bubble Map: Comparing and Contrasting Carrots
              and Oranges   86

List of Tables

Table 2.1   Domains of Child Development and Early Learning   23
Table 3.1   *Goldilocks and the Three Bears* Metacognitive Analysis   37
Table 3.2   Science and Mathematics Quick Content Correlations   45
Table 3.3   Productive Questioning Guides and Facilitates Sorting
             Biodegradable and Non-Biodegradable Items   52
Table 3.4   Productive Questioning Guides and Facilitates the Analysis
             of Motion Items   54

Foreword

I recently served on a panel where I was asked whether I thought how children are learning today will prepare them for the needs of the 21st century. I responded that the pertinent question is not one that asks whether our children are *learning* what will prepare them for the realities of the 21st century. Instead, the most urgent question is whether *how children are being taught* will, in fact, prepare them for the realities of a growing global interconnection and interdependency. This intersection has been made ever more apparent by the current pandemic, the effects of greed on the environment, and cyber-attacks, just to name a few. These realities have made all the more apparent and pressing the dire need for our children to be taught in ways that will develop the acuity and social-emotional skills that will prepare them to work cooperatively with people from diverse backgrounds and countries. Children rely on cognitive skills as they innovate, solving complex problems and global issues. The foundation of the teaching they should experience requires cognitive strategies that stimulate the development of foresight and the use of artificial intelligence that enable them to not only analyze and think critically, but to hypothesize, theorize, innovate, and even revolutionize to bring solutions for radical change where needed.

Generation Alpha is "the first to be born entirely within the 21st century. They are described by their diversity in key areas, including their race and ethnicity, family structure and family finances" (Annie E. Casey Foundation, 2020). Current findings from cognitive and neuroscience research have helped substantiate that children's brains are predisposed for the type of acuity, intellectual processing, executive functioning, and goal-directed behaviors needed to thrive and flourish in today's global world. Our young children of *advantaged means* are enabled to amplify and strengthen this predisposition through the fortune of being born into the world with access to the voice of Siri, Alexa, and the assistance of Google. By the age of 2 years, young children have learned how to manipulate a tablet, have been exposed to a multitude of information each day, and know how to filter this information to address their needs and interests, using technology for communication and play.

But what about those children who are not from advantaged backgrounds? The pandemic did more than just illustrate the fragility of our health care system and the consequences for wellness and well-being within our interconnected global community. COVID has monumentally impacted learning for all our young children across diverse communities. The relegated remote instruction was largely devoid of the type of experiences young children need to stimulate, elicit, and nurture their innate capacity for cognitive processing—requisite skills for literacy development and overall academic growth were stymied around the country (The 74, December 5, 2022). Children who were less advantaged and already struggling academically due to the lack of access to computers and technology prior to COVID fell even further behind with lost or limited instruction. The pernicious impact of COVID on our young children at the critical, formative stage of their development was exacerbated by the trauma they lived through as they witnessed the emotional and physical impact of the virus on their primary adults and caregivers—including the death of many—or the dark despair of some that resulted in homicide. The bereavement rates of our young children around the country spiked 25% in 2022 (The 74, November 28, 2022). This trauma, still experienced by our young children, causes the emission of the stress hormone cortisol in the brain, stifling their comprehension and causing regions of their brain associated with executive functioning and goal-directed behaviors to degenerate, contributing to cognitive and learning impairments.

This deleterious situation is far from hopeless. Jean Piaget's eminent disciple and cognitive scientist, Reuven Feuerstein, proved almost a century ago that impairments in academic learning due to trauma or debilitating conditions that cause cognition to under-function can be mitigated when students are provided with explicit, cognitive mediation, intervention strategies, and 21st-century cognitive tools such as Thinking Maps!

Thinking Maps' metacognitive framework fortifies the regions of the brain associated with executive functioning and goal-directed behaviors, accelerating intellectual development, diffusing the impact of trauma while innately nurturing high intellectual performance. They are tools that enable teachers to engage students in the metacognitive processing that supports and strengthens the neural and cognitive patterns children's brains rely on for making connections between new information and their schema of understanding, enabling them to conceptualize ideas and make new meanings necessary for higher-order thinking, literacy, and accelerated, adaptive learning.

That the research and applications of the Thinking Maps in this book validates their power is clear, comprehensive, and inspiring! They substantiate my own profound experience in using the TMaps for more

than 30 years as the fulcrum for my pedagogy to mediate the learning potential of students for giftedness and the power of the Thinking Maps for demonstrating that giftedness! As pedagogical gifts, Thinking Maps enable us to be the teachers needed to confidently guide and optimize the innate potential of our young Generation Alpha learners for high levels of learning and contribution, not only to survive, but to thrive, flourish, contribute, and where needed, revolutionize for globally interconnected and interdependent radical change in the 21st century.

—Yvette Jackson, Ed.D.

REFERENCES

Annie E. Casey Foundation. (2020, November 4). *What is Generation Alpha?* Annie E. Casey Blog. https://www.aecf.org/blog/what-is-generation-alpha

The 74. (2022, November 28). *Historic rise in child bereavement as COVID, drugs and guns claim parents' lives.* The 74 Blog. https://www.the74million.org/article/historic-rise-in-child-bereavement-as-covid-drugs-and-guns-claim-parents-lives/

The 74. (2022, December 5). *Schools face "urgency gap" on pandemic recovery: 5 takeaways from the new study.* The 74 Blog. https://www.the74million.org/article/schools-face-urgency-gap-on-pandemic-recovery-5-takeaways-from-new-study/

Acknowledgments

First and foremost, we want to extend our sincerest gratitude and appreciation to Hortencia Piña, an Educational Consultant with Thinking Maps, Inc. Since 2007, Hortencia has conducted teacher trainings nationwide with Pre-K–12 educators and administrators with a focus on early childhood and bilingual education. Hortencia's firsthand experiences, insights, and expertise have proven invaluable and indispensable in helping to guide and inform the organization, framework, language, and examples used in this book. We greatly appreciate the time, effort, and support that Hortencia graciously dedicated toward the completion of this book. Her edits, feedback, and recommendations on how to best illustrate and explain to educators how they can effectively and efficiently implement TMaps with young children within diverse, inclusive Pre-K–2 settings proved critical and essential to final product. We wholeheartedly thank her for her many contributions that have strengthened our book beyond measure.

We want to take this opportunity to likewise express our sincere gratitude to Geoff Suddreth, the vice president and general manager at Thinking Maps, Inc., for his assistance and support. Geoff's prompt attention and willingness to share published training manuals, the online gallery of teacher-submitted maps, and his overall encouragement and enthusiasm toward this effort are greatly appreciated. We believe that this book, in turn, will be a central resource to help prepare educators in Pre-K–2 settings to effectively implement TMaps with young children in ways that strengthen and enrich their teaching practices in developmentally appropriate ways while enhancing, improving, and maximizing children's learning and development.

Examples of engaging, dynamic TMaps actively implemented with young children would not be possible without the passion, determination, and commitment by teachers, administrators, and professionals who recognize the teaching and learning value of Thinking Maps with the full range of young learners in both formal and informal settings. Dr. Mary Palmer, the director of Campus Child Care Programs at Southwest Tennessee Community College, welcomed Dr. Counsell's early childhood candidates at the University of Memphis to conduct early STEM investigations and early language and literacy activities with young children at both the Macon Cove and Union Avenue campus centers. Implementing TMaps not only benefited children as they participated but also provided critical opportunities for teacher candidates to develop their own teaching practices, as they strived to connect constructivist theory to practice. These experiences likewise granted preschool teachers access to observe and to learn how to use a variety of high-quality, evidence-based practices like TMaps to help deepen and enrich discussions and conversations they have with children. Some of the photos featured in our book include Khayla Jennings, a former early childhood candidate, who implemented TMaps with children at the Union campus center. Today, Khayla is a J.D. (Juris Doctor) candidate in the Cecil C. Humphreys School of Law at the University of Memphis, scheduled to graduate in May 2023. We know she will continue to support Black children, families, and communities.

Similarly, another early childhood professional, Felicia Peat, has provided multiple opportunities for early childhood candidates at the UoM to use TMap activities with young children within a variety of informal settings. Dr. Counsell coordinated early childhood candidates' STEM investigations with Felicia at the Children's Museum of Memphis when she was the director of Education and Outreach, and during afterschool programs at local elementary schools such as the Dexter K–8 School in Cordova,

xvi   Acknowledgments

after Felicia became the Education and Outreach Manager of Kids Programming at the WKNO Public Broadcasting Station in Memphis. We thank Felicia Peat and Dr. Mary Palmer for their continued enthusiasm and ongoing support with promoting high-quality materials and activities like TMaps to maximize young children's learning and development in Memphis and the surrounding area.

A former early childhood candidate and the 2017 H. E. Rumble Outstanding Teacher Candidate of the Year, Kristal Rolfe-Fields has continued to implement TMap activities as a kindergarten teacher in the Bartlett School District. With permission from her school principal, Page Watson, Kristal has graciously shared classroom photos of her kindergartners participating in small-group TMap activities at Bartlett Elementary School. In addition to her classroom photos, Kristal has kindly agreed to allow us to showcase photos of a large Circle Map she used with her own sons at home to help brainstorm possible menu items they could choose from for breakfast, further promoting her sons' decision making, voice, and agency during family routines. We are impressed with and commend Kristal's continued interest and application of TMap thinking processes to support and promote children's learning and development at home and school.

Finally, we want to thank Kristen Counsell French for her willingness to share the TMaps that she created in 1st grade on the book cover and included in the discussion of the "All About Me" unit study. Today, Kristen has an undergraduate degree in microbiology and a master's degree in biochemistry and animal physiology. She works in cancer research.

Introduction

Can I Use Thinking Maps With Young Children? Yes, You Can!

I recall one day when I was discussing the different food groups with my preschool class as a parent volunteer looked on. We used a large Tree Map to classify the food items according to their corresponding food group. As we identified and discussed the various items and children eagerly took turns placing items on the map, I noticed that the parent looked sad. I thought she was close to tears.

After circle time ended and children went to different centers to work independently, I asked the mother if everything was okay and if she was upset by the learning activity. On the contrary, she said she was thrilled to see the rich language and vocabulary used by the children and the higher-order thinking used as they participated in the Thinking Maps activity. She said the learning activity helped to explain the language explosion she was witnessing in her 4-year-old son. At the same time, she said it saddened her greatly to realize how much her older daughter missed out in her very different preschool experience using a curriculum and activities that did not include Thinking Maps.

The Tree Map used in this example is a hierarchy that unveils in a visual form what often remains on "word walls" and in linear text or as verbally described by teachers and parents. So how is using a simple tree diagram an example of "higher order"? Because young children begin to see learning in the underlying language, and across content area disciplines there are rich thinking patterns of information in a range of different forms that ground how we make sense of the world. An apple, an orange, and a banana are not simply disconnected bits of information-content knowledge but are part of a larger picture of the conceptual patterns that exist beneath the physical forms: fruits, vegetables, and food groups are all categories under the broad category of "living things we eat." Thus a 4-year-old

child begins to *see* groups; they begin to form mental classifications and to see and construct hierarchies in the same way a scientist builds a taxonomy to better understand the world around us.

First conceived by David Hyerle in 1986 as a language of interdependent visual-verbal-spatial cognitive patterning tools, Thinking Maps® provide an instructional and learning visual framework for teachers and learners (Hyerle 1988–1993, 1990, 1993, 1995, 1996, 2000; Hyerle, Curtis, & Alper, 2004). Based on cognitive science research, models of thinking, and educational programs, Hyerle expanded and transformed Upton's (1960) six cognitive skills into a metacognitive framework that is most explicitly captured and conveyed by the current eight Thinking Maps. The eight Thinking Maps (TMaps) are a unified visual language with eight fundamental cognitive skills: (1) defining in context (Circle Map); (2) describing attributes (Bubble Map); (3) comparing and contrasting (Double-Bubble Map); (4) classifying (Tree Map); (5) part–whole spatial reasoning (Brace Map); (6) sequencing (Flow Map); (7) cause-and-effect reasoning (Multi-Flow Map); and (8) reasoning by analogy (Bridge Map) (Figure I.1).

Each of these visual maps, in isolation or in combination, is also used by teachers and learners with an optional visual Frame of Reference for facilitating reflective questions about how one literally draws out each map of knowledge from one's background experience and knowledge base.

Now understood as a visual language framework for learning, TMaps are neither linear nor hierarchical. Hyerle (2009) asserts that Thinking Maps should not be interpreted as a "comprehensive view of learning"; rather, they serve to identify "the coherence and interdependency of the eight

Figure I.1. Thinking Maps

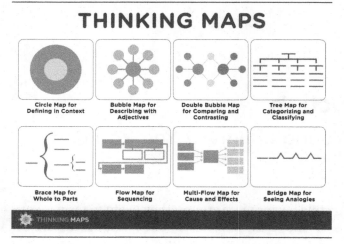

fundamental cognitive skills that ground thinking and learning" from more concrete to abstract, higher-order critical thinking (p. 119).

THINKING MAPS: INTEGRATING THREE TYPES OF VISUAL TOOLS

On a global level, Thinking Maps have been defined as a synthesis of three types of visual tools that educators and even businesspeople have used for generations: mind-mapping/brainstorming webs, graphic organizers, and thinking-process tools such as concept mapping. During his teaching with the Bay Area Writing Project in Oakland, California, and as he was developing the Thinking Maps language, David became intrigued by different types of visual tools, finally writing comprehensive books on the theory, practice, and degree of effectiveness of these tools in *Visual Tools for Constructing Knowledge* (Hyerle, 1996). He later revised and updated that work with current research connected to practice as a central theme for 21st-century learning in the text *Visual Tools for Transforming Information Into Knowledge* (Hyerle, 2009).

David found through research and practice in classrooms that each type of visual tool offers useful ways of visually accessing knowledge. He also found that each kind of visual tool also has some limitations that could not be overlooked.

Mind-Mapping techniques that surfaced in the early 1970s facilitated flexible, open-minded thinking often used during pre-writing processes, yet they lacked the consistent structure and deeper levels of complexity required for today's classrooms.

The now familiar "graphic organizers" that exploded in use during the 1980s and 1990s helped students more consistently organize large amounts of information and scaffold their thinking, but they failed when they become static, blackline masters focused on isolated content tasks selected by the teacher rather than initiated by the learner. These ubiquitous visual tools are what David defined as "task-specific" organizers because they typically focus on a specific content task and are often confined to the task at hand rather than easily transferable across disciplines.

A third kind of visual tool, "thinking-process" maps, are based on facilitating well-defined thinking processes. Two of these forms, concept mapping and systems diagramming, richly convey complex interdependencies in concepts and systems, respectively. Embedded in the strengths of these two models are also limitations: These developmental models integrate visuals and are each dependent on one form of visually structured knowledge: hierarchical forms for concept mapping and feedback loops for systems diagrams. This leads to an underrepresentation of other thinking processes. In addition, in practice, the translation of these complex models is often daunting for students and teachers alike.

Thinking Maps, to a significant degree, as we shall explore in depth in Chapter 1, are an integration of these three distinct types of visual tools. The combined practical, theoretical, and critical attributes of these different types of visual tools have informed the continuing evolution of TMaps into a 21st-century language for learning. By synthesizing many of the best qualities of these other types of visual tools, TMaps have evolved from the generative quality of brainstorming webs, the organizing structure of graphic organizers, and the deep cognitive processing found in concept maps.

If we accept that Thinking Maps provide an effective language framework that promotes overall learning and cognition, then would it also make sense to introduce this framework to our youngest learners sooner rather than later to promote their learning and cognitive development? While TMaps have been implemented across the entire K–16 educational spectrum, and after professional development, in many different countries, this book focuses on implementing TMaps with our youngest learners (ages 3–8) in preschool through 2nd-grade educational settings.

The typical notions and applications of webbing and mapping as graphic organizers as preformed structures for visually guiding content learning for brainstorming purposes conjure images of paper-and-pencil tasks as learners and educators discuss and write key concepts, ideas, and mental relationships pertaining to a specific topic or theme, such as the different food groups, as described above. In this traditional sense, a learner's ability to successfully convey their knowledge and understanding using a wide array of visual tools (Hyerle, 1996) relies in large part on their language and literacy skill development. Learners often find creating and completing Thinking Maps to be an enjoyable and successful experience. This is because TMaps reflect different types of thinking, and learners slowly and surely take charge of how they are visually, verbally, and spatially mapping, for example, different types of fruit; sequencing the plot of a story; showing the causes and effects of behavior in the classroom; and comparing a triangle and a square. If TMaps rely heavily on reading and writing skills, how can they be utilized by younger children and struggling learners?

What and how young learners are thinking are most often expressed and shared at home and in classrooms through verbal and written modes of communication. As a visual language framework, Thinking Maps offer an additional way for learners to represent their ideas: by visually mapping their fundamental patterns of thinking. Rather than limiting the use of Thinking Maps as paper-and-pencil learning tasks and activities, as offered by previously published materials and used for implementing this visual language framework across whole school faculties (i.e., Draw Your Thinking, Pre-K–K; Map Your Thinking, grades 1–2; and Show Your Thinking, grades 2–3), the authors offer a wide range of strategies, activities, and materials for implementing TMaps (as cognitive frameworks of understanding) and the metacognitive strategy that each map promotes and supports in ways that are developmentally appropriate with young children.

Shelly Counsell first encountered Thinking Maps as a teaching framework and learning tool during a professional learning workshop as a Pre-K teacher at an Orlando public school in 1998. She has continued to use and promote them throughout her career as a teacher-educator in her early childhood methods courses. Her earliest efforts to increase young children's active engagement with each map's intentional framework of mental relationships (such as the Double-Bubble Map's focus on comparing and contrasting similarities and differences) led her to the realization that using physically tangible maps, written word labels, photos, pictures, and actual objects dramatically increase young children's accessibility and active engagement with the different maps and metacognitive strategies. Guided by her early childhood and special education preparation and experience, she quickly understood that children's hands-on and minds-on exploration of concrete objects enhances their ability to connect and construct concepts, ideas, and mental relationships to their current and increasing schema of understanding (e.g., comparing and contrasting a cat and a dog using a Double-Bubble Map).

WHY EARLY CHILDHOOD?

Since children's intelligence, according to Piaget (1971) "organizes the world as it organizes itself," what better way to promote mental organizations than using Thinking Maps? As such, children's frameworks of understanding (their interrelated cognitive schema) based on rule formation are internally constructed through their actions on objects in the world (Counsell & Sander, 2016; DeVries & Sales, 2011; DeVries & Zan, 2012). Schemas essentially represent "intelligence in action" (Goleman, 1985, p. 85), and children can more readily demonstrate and express their current and growing schemas using maps and the related metacognitive strategies. The mental operations identified by Piaget and early childhood development research has focused on the same processes that define TMaps such as classification, sequencing, part–whole, compare–contrast, and cause–effect.

The Brain as Pattern Detector

After all, the brain, as suggested by Caine and Caine (1994) and others, is a pattern detector (Duncan, 2010; Healy & Hurly, 2004; Holland & Kensinger, 2010; Mattson, 2014). The physical brain, as we now know, is continuously networking incoming sensory information (attributes), sequentially relaying information, and reinforcing and pruning informing into hierarchies, all the while redirecting and comparing new information to that which is one's storehouse of knowledge and experiences. Detected patterns are used to guide and inform mental relationships. Hence, "the brain makes sense of the world by constructing or mapping patterns of the world" (Hyerle, 2009, p. 27). TMaps in turn, serve as visual frameworks used by children to graphically display newly formed schema of understanding. Teachers, in turn, can use children's current schematic understanding revealed by Thinking Maps as a formative assessment to further guide and inform developmentally appropriate instructional practices and learning experiences.

Thinking in Constructivist Classrooms

Constructivist classrooms provide young children with important opportunities to build content knowledge through active exploration, making sense of their surroundings, using knowledge and understanding to design and create something new—activities involving inquiry and engineering design (Brooks, 2011; Schunn, 2009; Yasar et al., 2006). With confirmation from neuroscience that the brain learns best by organizing semantic information into networks and maps (De Deyne & Storms, 2008; Griffiths et al., 2007; Yee et al., 2018), what better way to teach children to think about ideas and organize and express their ideas in ways that are meaningful and relevant than to capitalize on mapping processes that complement brain networking?

TMaps with young children can easily integrate drawings, pictures, or actual objects with words (oral and written) to form a rich mental bond within the full range of diverse learners' brains and minds to help remember and recall relevant information. This "bond" is thus internally constructed by the young child, and the TMaps provide a rich and dynamic visual and spatial arrangement that complements and reinforces verbal and mathematical languages. This process helps children conceptualize and transform their ideas, understanding, and interpretations into meaningful visual displays. Since the brain's visual processing is critical and instantaneous (Lindsay, 2020; Trafton, 2014) and, as noted above, pre-structured in processes such as hierarchies and sequences, TMaps effectively tap into the brain/mind capacity. This capacity reinforces children's memory by actively engaging visual stimuli with meaning, helping children to form, connect, and expand mental concepts and relationships (visual-spatial-verbal schemas or mental frameworks).

THINKING MAPS AS A LEARNING, TEACHING, AND ASSESSMENT FRAMEWORK

Cooperative learning is identified by Marzano et al. (2001) as one of the nine strategies that directly impact learner achievement. Thinking Maps can be utilized in a variety of learning arrangements, including independent, small-group, and whole-group settings. Using an ideal teaching and learning framework during cooperative learning, children gain new insights and multiple perspectives, expanding their own schema of understanding as they construct mental relationships and mental frameworks together. As young children work together during the mapping process, they are encouraged to challenge their own assumptions, to recognize new patterns, to make new connections, and to visualize the unknown (Barkman, 2021; Bor, 2012; Kurzweil, 2012; Wandersee, 1990).

TMaps encourage children to actively and strategically engage problem-solving strategies and skills involved in higher-order critical thinking. Hyerle (2009) notes five essential qualities required to ensure that TMaps are infinitely expandable and capable of being used simultaneously: (1) graphically consistent, (2) flexible, (3) developmental, (4) integrative, and (5) reflective. We will further explore these five attributes of Thinking Maps in Chapter 1. Together, these qualities increase the likelihood that TMaps will help children develop more complex, higher-order critical thinking such as problem solving, evaluating, analyzing, and thinking systematically as well as the creative processes of developmental learning.

As children develop socially, emotionally, and cognitively, with teacher guidance, they move beyond using each Thinking Map as an isolated tool, and naturally begin to orchestrate the use of multiple TMaps together. For is it not enough, to expand on the example above, to classify an apple as a fruit using a Tree Map? We want young learners to independently compare and contrast fruit using a Double-Bubble Map; to sequence the life cycle of an apple with a Flow Map; and to understand the cause–effect relationship that eating a piece of fruit has on a healthy diet as well as the longer-term effects of eating fruit regularly. All in a nutshell, a foundation for learning includes developing children's ability to orchestrate their own thinking about whatever they are exploring and to see the patterns that connect into meaningful learning.

Thinking Maps in Action

TMap activities and materials used to support and promote young children's metacognitive strategy development advanced by the authors in this book utilize a very practical and pragmatic approach based on concepts and skills promoted by most early childhood preschool and elementary curricula programs. In each chapter are many applications and specific activities described and designed in ways that intentionally create highly engaging, stimulating, and enjoyable teaching and learning contexts for educators and young children alike.

Thinking Maps Are Not Limited to Classrooms

Although the maps have been developed for use in classroom settings, this does not mean they are not relevant or useful in settings outside of school. Parents, counselors, therapists, tutors, daycare providers, recreational leaders, boys and girls clubs, children's museum directors, librarians, and a variety of local and national organizations (e.g., Easter Seals, YMCA/YWCA, Big Brothers and Big Sisters, Scouts) can use maps in creative ways to support learning activities with young children.

In any case, it is imperative that professionals who use TMaps with children do not minimize these experiences as merely fun diversions from the daily tasks required by scripted curricula worksheets and workbooks. Instead, maximum learning outcomes

for cognition and other developmental domains and across curricular content requires professionals to mindfully use TMap metacognitive strategies systematically within a variety of learning group arrangements. The more children are exposed to maps outside of school, the opportunity to improve their metacognitive processing will likely increase, while interacting with academic content, concepts, and skills within real-world contexts and applications. Key terminology and definitions needed to develop a strong foundational understanding and pedagogical application of TMaps with young children is provided in the appendix.

Chapter 1, "Bringing Thinking Maps to Life," describes in great detail how the authors' recommended approach to using tangible maps with movable objects and visual materials supports our youngest learners' developmental progression and learning trajectory across domains and academic content areas. TMaps allow for child-directed learning within a child-centered approach that encourages active engagement with ongoing dialogues and questioning, further supporting social-emotional learning as children become increasingly open to each other's patterns of thinking during cooperative learning groups.

Thinking Maps have been used widely as a metacognitive framework to support teachers' instruction (and children's learning) across curricular content areas, to facilitate STEM concepts and skills, and to promote language development and instruction. This teaching framework is organized according to the eight TMaps (Hyerle & Alper, 2011) described earlier. These maps provide teachers with hands-on graphic, schematic mental and conceptual framework used to help children draw secondary abstract concepts in real time to support and promote their learning and development. Each map empowers children to directly visualize their ideas as they make sense of content using the eight fundamental thinking processes.

During the teaching-learning-assessment process, map-making serves four basic purposes: Maps help teachers to (1) challenge children's assumptions, (2) recognize new patterns, (3) make new connections, and (4) visualize the unknown (Hyerle, 2009, p. 13). As detailed in Chapter 2, "Thinking Maps Across Developmental Domains," and Chapter 3, "Thinking Maps Across Academic Content Areas," the authors provide multiple examples of how to use TMaps to enhance and improve instructional teaching practices and increase learner outcomes.

Diversity and Inclusion Considerations

An accessible curriculum is one in which all aspects of the curriculum (i.e., the environment, the goals, the content, the instructional methods and interactions, the assessments, and the toys/materials) invite active participation of *all* children regardless of disability or special needs (Counsell, 2009; Counsell & Sander, 2016). Children who struggle academically or exhibit developmental delays benefit significantly from maximum active engagement rather than predominant teacher-directed instruction (Bodovski & Farkas, 2007).

As one of the leaders of the National Urban Alliance for Effective Education, Yvette Jackson (2011) explains, "Our mission is to substantiate in the public schools of urban America the irrefutable belief in the capacity of all children to reach high levels of learning and thinking demanded by our ever-changing global community. Our focus is on altering educators' perceptions and expectations of underperforming urban children, and this comes right out of my early interest in mediating learning" (p. 52).

According to Jackson, teachers who acknowledge an existing gap between themselves and their students are experiencing a "cultural gap" that separates their Frame of Reference and language from those used by their students. Any effort to bridge the gap between teachers and their underachieving urban learners must consider three interconnected factors: (1) addressing the fear that teachers have in not being able to address the needs of their underachieving learners so that they can meet standards; (2) addressing learners' needs by shifting the focus from what is taught (content) to how learning happens (cognition, metacognition, process) and what affects it; and (3) providing teachers and learners with a language that enables them to communicate with each other, building the mutual respect and relationships that are vital to *all* learners.

The authors share a strong commitment and passion about the powerful impact that TMaps hold for the full range of diverse learners. While Chapter 4, "Thinking Maps Promote Democratic Learning Communities with Full Community Membership,"

provides elaborate examples to clearly illustrate how teachers can easily scaffold learning according to individual learners' zone of proximal development using TMaps within inclusive, diverse settings, this same view is consistent and integrated throughout the book. Important developmental and diversity considerations discussed include universal design for learning (UDL), differentiated instruction, as well as equity, accessibility, and community membership. As illustrated throughout the book, TMaps exemplify both a culturally sensitive and responsive as well as a universally designed practice. The use of TMaps is thus an ideal practice easily adapted for use for a full range of diverse learners. For this reason, all references to children therefore entail the full range of diverse learners, including children with disabilities.

Just as Thinking Maps can transform educators' teaching practice that, in turn, changes learners' educational experience from passive onlooker to actively engaged, they can likewise provide authentic, meaningful, and purposeful data demonstrating children's learning and understanding. Chapter 5, "Thinking Maps Provide Authentic Formative Assessment and Documentation," elaborates on the potential of TMaps as a framework for formative, summative, performance-based assessments based on individual, small-group, and whole-group documentation demonstrating what children know and understand. The authors demonstrate how individual maps completed by children are ideal permanent products that illustrate skill development and understanding as valid evidence for overall performance and key contributions to individual child portfolios.

Not only can Thinking Maps serve as an important source of documented performance of individual learners or groups, they can also provide important information, as suggested by Hyerle (2000), as self-assessments used by learners. Learners can mindfully read, interpret, and reflect on their own thinking about concepts, ideas, and relationships explored using the different TMaps.

The effective implementation of any educational curriculum, strategy, methodology, or approach relies heavily on the preparation, expertise, and skill development of the educator. While this resource has been organized and written pragmatically, offering practical examples within a comprehensive, research-based vision of how to directly facilitate early childhood development, ongoing training and preparation are recommended in order to fully enhance and deepen educators' skills and usage and successful implementation of TMaps with young learners. A whole-school approach, beginning in Pre-K, supports the critical early foundation for continuous metacognitive learning and development throughout the school years and beyond.

Finally, the book comes full circle in Chapter 6, "The Science Underlying Thinking Maps with Young Children," by outlining various research and theoretical foundations for using TMaps with young children (Pre-K through 2nd grade). The authors explain how Thinking Maps promote children's development of habits of mind (Costa & Kallick, 2000) and executive function (EF) skills (including inhibitory control needed for self-regulation) that are critical for kindergarten readiness and later academic achievement. As child-directed and child-centered framework for learning, TMaps simultaneously provide a developmentally appropriate teaching framework and practices that are easily aligned with local and state learning standards across academic content areas.

CHAPTER 1

Bringing Thinking Maps to Life

Young learners benefit greatly from materials and activities that are both visually stimulating and include "hands-on" manipulatives that actively engage them in the learning process. To satisfy these criteria, I designed large Thinking Maps on colored plastic tablecloths (purchased at the Dollar Store) using permanent black marker, each color symbolizing a specific map (e.g., circle map—red; brace map—blue). Real-life items, plastic models, or replicas are used for children to place on the maps along with word labels that identify and describe each item. (S. Counsell, personal communication, February 15, 2000)

The above testimonial was written by Shelly as a Pre-K Teacher at Palm Lake Elementary, Orange County Public Schools (OCPS) in Orlando, and appeared in the OCPS Thinking Maps Committee, Professional Development Services' *Thinking Maps News* (2000). As suggested above, young children are ready and eager to learn at the outset. In order to fully capitalize on young children's eagerness to engage with the people, activities, and materials they encounter in their formal and informal educational settings, it is imperative to prepare educators to engage children in rich content and language experiences that help to lay the foundation for school success and eventual workplace (Brenneman et al., 2009; Clements and Sarama, 2009). Educators use three categories of knowledge when teaching subject-matter content (Wilson et al., 2014): (1) general pedagogical knowledge, (2) content knowledge, and (3) common content knowledge. General pedagogical knowledge refers to general teaching strategies (e.g., Thinking Maps) that have application across academic subjects. In contrast, content knowledge pertains to the subject matter itself, and common content knowledge is the specific concepts and skills learners are expected to learn (Institute of Medicine and National Research Council, 2015).

In other words, effective instruction and curricula (like maps) scaffold children's thinking through both creative invention and skill practice while challenging them to explain their strategies, reasoning, and understanding (Hiebert, 1999). Thinking Maps (TMaps) support teachers' explicit instruction of concepts by making the mental connections among facts, procedures, concepts, and processes visible to learners—connections leading to higher achievement, especially when child centered (Clements & Sarama, 2012; Hiebert & Grouws, 2007). Since concepts and skills develop simultaneously (Verschaffel et al., 2007) maps serve to explicitly and fully develop and utilize children's linguistic skills and cognitive processes as they construct verbal-visual-spatial mental relationships based on new concepts and content knowledge.

LEARNING TRAJECTORIES AND DEVELOPMENTAL PROGRESSIONS

It is a widely accepted tenet in early childhood education that all young children learn according to developmental sequences of typical accomplishments within and across age ranges. Although predictable, a developmental continuum is not rigid. Research-based developmental and learning continua are the basis for planning the scope and sequence of a curriculum.

While similar to a developmental continuum, a learning continuum or trajectory focuses on sequences of knowledge or skill in specific content area, such as math (Sarama & Clements, 2009). Children progress through increasingly sophisticated and complex levels of thinking as they learn about a topic of study. When educators develop a mastery of content knowledge combined with content learning and levels of thinking, children learn to effectively use skills fluently and flexibly with superior conceptual understanding.

As important developmental paths, learning trajectories contain three essential parts: (1) a goal, (2) a developmental progression, and (3) instructional activities (National Mathematics Advisory Panel, 2008). From this stance, TMaps provide an explicit learner-centered framework and grounded instructional activities that further help educators to accurately identify learning goals according to developmental progressions in developmentally appropriate ways.

As a result, developmentally appropriate practices are guided by developmental sequences and children's zone of proximal development. Scaffolding children's learning is largely informed by educators' careful observations and guided questioning used to check for, and to help facilitate, children's understanding. Educators use this "horizon knowledge" about how children learn and develop content to guide and inform how the content is most effectively and coherently taught over time. Additionally, educators use "pedagogical content knowledge" about specific content topics with an awareness of common misconceptions as well as constructs and skills that children may find particularly challenging or motivating (Wilson et al., 2014).

Rather than approach academic content and subject-matter concepts in isolated silos, TMaps help educators to integrate concepts and skills across domains and subjects in ways that are meaningful, purposeful, and relevant to learners. For example, a thoughtful selection of children's books such as *Everyone Poops* by Taro Gomi during a study unit on mammals can help children explore concepts and relationships that are scientific (e.g., animal groups, food chains, digestion) and mathematical (e.g., size, height, weight; quantity; measurement; sequence; seriation). Children can use a Circle Map to brainstorm everything they know about mice (Figure 1.1); a Bubble Map to use adjectives that describe mice (Figure 1.2); and a Flow Map to sequence a food chain (Figure 1.3), just to name a few.

This kind of integrated curriculum mindfully promotes content vocabulary and other language and literacy competencies with increased grammatical complexity as children independently reproduce narratives and use inferential reasoning (Peterson & French, 2008; Raudenbush, 2009; Sarama et al., 2012) as they comprehend, interpret, and summarize what they read using maps. TMaps, as a framework, offer a coherent, fundamental, integrated cognitive vocabulary using visual-verbal-spatial representations of specific thinking patterns that explicitly visualize the underlying logic of these processes, such as hierarchical, comparative, and cause–effect structures.

Figure 1.1. Circle Map: Brainstorming About Mice

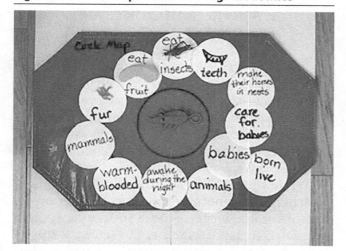

Figure 1.2. Bubble-Map: Adjectives Describing Mice

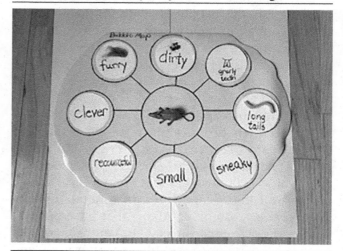

Figure 1.3. Flow Map: Sequencing a Food Chain Including Mice

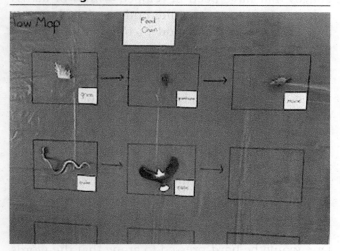

Just as mathematical knowledge and reasoning rely heavily on logic, scientific knowledge and reasoning rely tremendously on observation and experimentation (IOM & NRC, 2015). A case in point, van den Heuvel-Panhuizen and Elia (2012) found that young children who engaged in mathematics-related storybook reading, participated in book discussions, and played with related math materials developed stronger mathematical dispositions than a control group—math and science dispositions that can be further enhanced and supported using maps.

Introducing Thinking Maps as a Pattern Language

Psychologists, cognitive scientists, and educators have richly researched the eight fundamental cognitive processes, as described in more detail below, reaching far back into the early history of modern education. These eight structures were identified by Jean Piaget as "mental operations" that are foundational. These cognitive processes are used in isolation and in combination as we assimilate and accommodate new content and concepts. They are with us as we shift from concrete to abstract thinking. Mental operations such as comparisons, categorization, seriation, causality, and whole–part reasoning are with us our entire lives and develop as "content knowledge" and conceptual understandings become more complex.

Thinking Maps, as a pattern language of cognitive processes, are a way for learners to become conscious of and to transfer these mental operations into any learning environment, from early childhood to the adult workplace. Teachers use the TMaps to convey, facilitate, and mediate thinking and learning as every learner becomes more fluent with the maps as a language. In single classrooms and across whole schools over multiple years, students are generating ever more complex applications of single maps by their own hands and creating unique configurations of multiple maps together in response to the content and concepts they are learning. Of course, several of the graphic primitives have been used for a long time to help generate and communicate processes, such as the Flow Map (or flowchart) for sequencing and cycles, the Tree Map for conceptualizing hierarchies and taxonomies, and the Brace Map for diagramming the anatomy of the major and minor parts of the human body. What is *new* about Thinking Maps is not the idea of dynamic graphic primitives (all languages are built on this premise), but that there is a coherent, interdependent, and universal array of thinking processes that are used in orchestration by students and teachers as a common visual language for learning.

What Makes Thinking Maps a "Language"?

In the past, TMaps have been defined as a *model, an approach*, and simply as a *tool kit*. But these are inadequate terms for what is really a new, universal *language* for thinking and learning content within disciplines and for transdisciplinary concepts, projects, and communicating within classrooms. Thinking Maps, independently and/or together, comprise a language of visual tools based on fundamental cognitive processes showing content in patterns.

One analogy here may help. There are eight "parts of speech" in the English language that are distinct and used together in consistent and highly adaptive ways. Of course, not every sentence requires the use of all eight types of words. Thinking Maps convey meaning as the eight distinct cognitive processes are used interdependently. TMaps is a visual verbal language in which learners of any age can develop fluency, as with any adaptive language that is developed from the early years onward.

Becoming fluent with the language takes time as learners move from simple novice applications to expert uses. As documented in classrooms to boardrooms, TMaps, much like the English language or mathematical notation, are used at different levels of complexity as we mature. In the long term, learners become fluent with TMaps as a foundation for continuous cognitive development and high-quality collaboration as teachers and learners may say with confidence and clarity: *I see what you mean.*

Graphic Primitives

First and foremost, this language is grounded in and defined by eight *interdependent* cognitive processes we use daily as human beings to make sense of our world and through which we survive. Another key dimension of this language is the eight visual starting points, or graphic primitives, from which emerge unique patterns that are congruent, respectively, with each of the cognitive processes. For example, a simple box of the Flow Map for the universal process of sequencing is drawn as a starting point for visually showing simple "beginning, middle and end" stages in a story in pre-K to highly complex story narratives such as in the modern novel, or parallel processes on a computer.

It is clear that human beings are uniquely metacognitive, meaning that we can consciously reflect on *what* we are thinking and on *how* we are thinking. With Thinking Maps, all learners gain a visual-verbal language of cognition, thus enabling a deeper capacity to see, transfer, reflect upon, and improve their thinking abilities. As introduced in a comprehensive book, *Student Successes with Thinking Maps* (Hyerle, 2004), TMaps, in a nutshell, are a *pattern language*. Almost all languages and code (except spoken-only languages) have graphic primitives: 0–9 (plus operations such as +, −, and =) in mathematics, alphabetic systems such as the 27 letters in the English language (plus punctuation), and musical notation. Each of these languages is based on *unique graphic primitives* that are interdependent and combined in simple ways to create complex representations of ideas, emotions, analytic arguments, discoveries, and works of art. These symbols are arbitrary; they don't *mean* anything in how they look other than what *we* ascribe to them in our language community.

Thinking Maps are no different from other languages that have been developed within or across cultures: Languages are inherently *made* by humans and thus are arbitrary and incomplete, and have gray areas and sometimes ambiguous "rules" that govern daily usage in a language community. Yet, we agree as communities to use these imperfect languages because we find them useful for communication in our daily lives.

Interestingly, we have never had a language of cognition, or, more specifically, a language for generating patterns of thinking based on human cognitive structures. Certainly, our spoken and written and mathematical languages are all based on being able to represent our thinking, ideas, and concepts but *not* for explicitly representing thinking as patterns. One would be hard-pressed to argue that the words set in linear sequence found on this page actually *display* thinking patterns such as comparisons or categories, metaphors, or complex causal relationships. Our written languages have *embedded* within them all of these cognitive patterns, but they do not appear before your eyes right now on this page. The thinking patterns are embedded in the linearity of text, and you need to work a bit to dig them out.

Further, Thinking Maps complement and support the integration of all the languages we use in school, around the house, or at the workplace. As shown in this book, the maps directly support language acquisition, reading comprehension, writing processes, mathematical problem solving, and inquiry-based science. TMaps offer a language that combines symbols: All other symbols and pictorial representations may be used within each of the TMaps. Maybe the most obvious link to other languages pertains to how Thinking Maps function. From a blank page or computer screen, we can map iterations of basic cognitive patterns starting with simple graphics, much like we write out sentences on a blank tablet. This is possible because, as mentioned in the Introduction, there are five distinct qualities, or critical attributes, that give definition to TMaps as a language.

THE FIVE CRITICAL ATTRIBUTES OF THINKING MAPS

As noted above, by integrating several key characteristics of different types of visual tools, a language of cognitive patterns emerged in the form of Thinking Maps. TMaps are more consistently visual than "graphic organizers," as flexible as "Mind Mapping," as developmental and integrative as "Concept Mapping," and as reflective as "systems thinking" diagrams.

The graphic symbols of each Thinking Map become the simple visual starting point for generating complex maps, linking content together using a range of thinking processes into cohesive and coherent cognitive networks of meaning. Each of the eight TMaps is theoretically and practically grounded in an everyday fundamental cognitive process, or what is often called a "thinking skill."

Awareness of five critical attributes of Thinking Maps and a close look at just one of the eight maps (the Flow Map) will clarify how all the maps work and how they work together. For introducing these five attributes, we have used just the Flow Map (see Figure 1.3) for sequencing as an example that is reflected in each of the eight TMaps.

1. **Consistent.** The symbol grounding each map has a unique but consistent form that visually reflects the cognitive skill being defined. For example, the process of sequencing is represented by the Flow Map starting with one box and one arrow. This is the graphic primitive upon which the map is used to show linear concepts. Thus, a Flow Map might show just the three boxes, with key information written inside, showing the beginning, middle, and end of a story.

2. **Flexible.** The cognitive skill and the graphic primitive for each map lead to a flexibility in form and to the infinite number of ways the map can grow and be configured. A Flow Map of a story may start at the beginning but grow in complexity to show many stages and substages of the story. This map could be drawn rising from the bottom left to top right of the page, reflecting the rising action of a story.

3. **Developmental.** Because of the consistent graphic primitives and flexible use, any learner (at any age) may begin with a blank sheet of paper and expand the map to show their thinking. A Flow Map can be a few boxes long or evolve over time

to fill a whole page. The learner, and the content of the learning, determines the complexity of the map. Every learner, from early childhood on, can use the Flow Map to show what they know about a story and thus produce a different configuration of the content.

4. **Integrative.** There are two key dimensions of integration: thinking processes and content knowledge. First, all of the maps may be used and integrated together. Using the example of a story, a learner could use the Flow Map to show the plot, a Double-Bubble Map to show a comparison of characters, and then a Tree Map to identify the main ideas and supporting details. Multiple TMaps are used for solving multistep problems, for comprehending overlapping reading text structures, and for use during phases of the writing process. Second, the maps are used deeply within and across content areas. For example, the Flow Map is used for plot analysis in reading comprehension, order of operations in math, historical timelines in social studies, and studying recurring natural cycles in science.

5. **Reflective.** As a language, the maps unveil what and how one is thinking in patterns. Not only can the learner look down and reflect on the pattern of content, but the teacher also reflects on and informally assesses the content learning and thinking processes of the learner.

The definition and promise of Thinking Maps as a true language—as comparable to other graphic languages such as musical notation, mathematical numerals and operations, the English language, and combined languages such as scientific notation (using letters, numbers, and unique symbols)—has yet to be fully realized. As examples illustrate throughout this book, teachers and learners may use one TMap at a time or commit to learning how all eight TMaps and the Frame of Reference may be used and integrated together in a single lesson. Yet, there are many examples and documented applications around the world of how teachers and their students reach levels of fluency with TMaps that brings about significant growth. This growth is not just apparent in their increased content and conceptual knowledge. The growth is also visible in how they apply and improve their capacities to think and communicate using a new language of cognition.

Children's developmental progression in their thinking and understanding as they learn specific content expands and deepens while gaining competence and the levels and patterns of their thinking grow in complexity—a progression in complexity, sophistication, and abstraction that is also observed as children demonstrate their knowledge and understanding using TMaps across the grades. As a result, the development of any comprehensive, high-quality early learning curriculum requires well-qualified educators who are well prepared to employ all three components of learning trajectories, as noted by IOM and NRC (2015): subject-matter content, developmental progressions for each content area, and instructional tasks and strategies (like TMaps) that promote learning along learning trajectories and progressions. For example, cognitive processes such as hierarchical classification (using the Tree Map) is found in every content area silo and embedded within each child's learning progressions. As with each of the eight TMaps and frame, each visual representation becomes a tangible, visual scaffold for thought and language.

TMAPS TAP INTO PRIOR KNOWLEDGE AND EXPERIENCE

Even if young children encounter high-quality learning experiences in early childhood, the effects will not last indefinitely in later schooling of children's nascent learning trajectories without continual, progressive support (O'Connor et al., 2013, 2014). This is especially true when children attend poor-quality schools that assume low levels of knowledge, focus on lower-level skills, and set low expectations for different groups of learners (Engel et al., 2013). Just as there is the potential for a cumulative positive effect resulting from consecutive years of high-quality learning and instruction, there is the likelihood of a cumulative negative effect of low-quality learning and instruction, especially for potentially vulnerable groups, such as low-income populations (Akiba et al., 2007; Ballou et al., 2004; Darling-Hammond, 2006).

Never Assume What Children Do and Do Not Know

Well-prepared educators who provide high-quality instruction with young children in preschool and primary grades understand and appreciate that any new unit of study begins first with *determining*—not assuming (based on biased preconceptions of what children know or have experienced according to gender, age, social class, ethnicity, culture, etc.)—through observing and listening as children demonstrate and express what they already know and understand. In order for children to make sense of new information and experiences they encounter, they must draw on their prior knowledge and experience to see how the new experience and information fits into their existing knowledge. We often use the word "draw" in the above statement metaphorically; with TMaps young learners begin to draw their own ideas in visual thinking patterns.

If children easily connect new information with prior knowledge, they feel satisfied, which results in an inner state of balance that Piaget (1978) refers to as equilibrium. If children are unable to connect information to their prior knowledge, then the new information leads to an inner state of disturbance that Piaget further defines as disequilibrium. Disequilibrium plays a crucial and essential role during the learning process as children strive to acquire and construct new mental relationships. After all, it is the state of disequilibrium that compels the child to continue thinking and contemplating the new information and experience until they are able to make sense of it, and thus return to a state of equilibrium.

Brainstorming With K-W-Ls and Circle Maps

One familiar and widely accepted practice used by educators to initiate instruction by first determining children's prior knowledge is the K-W-L approach that first asks, "What do children already know?" Understanding children's prior knowledge is also a key aspect in determining the individual child's zone of proximal development that enables the educator to scaffold children's learning with developmentally appropriate experiences and intervention that build on their existing knowledge.

It is not uncommon to see preschool and primary grade teachers use K-W-Ls across the three phases of the Project Approach. The Project Approach encourages children to pursue projects on topics or subjects that interest them while eliminating mindless activities (such as coloring worksheets) that fail to promote academic or intellectual goals (Helm & Katz, 2011; Helm & Snider, 2020). Interest, according to Piaget (1981), is the fuel that drives the engine of mental activity. Hence, the Project Approach takes full advantage of children's interest as the driving force for teaching and learning.

Like the "K" that stands for what children already "know" in the K-W-L approach, the Circle Map is designed for brainstorming ideas or thoughts about a chosen topic and can easily be implemented during Phase 1 (Beginning) of the Project Approach. As in the case of the Circle Map about mice, described earlier (see Figure 1.1), the information that children include in the map reveals what children "already know" and understand. Not only does the Circle Map help teachers determine children's prior knowledge, it serves as a meaningful and authentic pre-assessment (prior to teaching new concepts, skills, and information); post-assessment (when children complete a follow-up Circle Map) at the end of the unit of study; and a self-assessment (as children compare their prior knowledge with learned knowledge).

Each of the other (seven) Thinking Maps may be used in isolation, or together, to conduct pre-assessments. For example, the Brace Map could be used to find out what students know about the physical parts of a mouse and/or the Bubble Map for identifying basic knowledge of the characteristics of mice. For a global assessment of general background knowledge, the Circle Map is a visual representation to which the Frame of Reference may be added, thus eliciting from learners how they know this information. What is known from seeing a real mouse? Did they see pictures of mice? Did they hear a story about the City Mouse and the Country Mouse? The cognitive processes as visual patterns "drawn out" in each map is then deepened by the metacognitive Frame of Reference and additional information from which teachers can assess prior knowledge.

During Phase 2 (Investigation) in the Project Approach, children's questions and problems begin to emerge as they explore and learn about the chosen topic. The more they learn, the more they want to know and understand, which can be framed and documented as the "W" that stands for "wonder" or "want to know" in the K-W-L. Children can use maps to stimulate their own thinking as they use each metacognitive strategy to ask questions and organize what they know into frameworks about what they are wondering about or trying to figure out.

Much like the "L" that stands for what children Learned in the K-W-L, a follow-up Circle Map (and some if not all of the other TMaps) can also help children reflect on the new insights and information they gained during Phase 3 (Culmination) of the Project Approach. Additional TMaps can likewise demonstrate learned concepts and information, like the Flow Map used to sequence a food chain that includes mice (see Figure 1.3) as described in the study unit on mammals.

THINKING MAPS EXEMPLIFIES UNIVERSALLY DESIGNED LEARNING (UDL)

The three UDL principles—(1) multiple means of representation, (2) multiple means of action and expression, (3) multiple means of engagement altogether—create flexible paths to learning for children. Inclusive and culturally responsive educators use multiple means of representation and expression to support learners' engagement, provide opportunities, and make informed decisions. The activities, materials, and strategies recommended in this book strive to satisfy the UDL principles by maximizing Thinking Maps as sensorial experiences with young children.

The importance of capitalizing on early sensorial experiences to promote the full range of diverse young children's learning and development (including children with disabilities) is another longstanding tenet in both early childhood and special education. When educators teach using single sensory instruction, information is often verbalized and received through children's auditory receptors. In multisensory teaching, also referred to as the VAKT (Visual, Auditory, Kinesthetic, Tactile) Approach, children receive and interpret information across the sensory modalities. Teaching with a multisensory approach is believed to strengthen neural pathways in the brain for more automatic retrieval of information (Kelly & Phillips, 2016).

A specific thought process translated into a visual-spatial-verbal pattern and corresponding cognitive vocabulary is represented by each TMap (Hyerle and Yeager, 2018). Each map's patterned framework help children to simultaneously connect the visual and auditory modalities. As such, each TMap's visual pattern (concrete image) aligns with the corresponding linguistic thought process (abstract concepts) that, in turn, help children to develop, expand, and deepen their comprehension and usage of the conceptual vocabulary and terminology, both expressively (verbally and written) and receptively (heard and read), during TMap activities. Much as we look at a road map, a Google map, or a geographic map, or even a map of the stars or neural networks using fMRIs, Thinking Maps offer a visual and spatial array of a child's thinking to our questions and adaptive projects—beyond the singular track of auditory presentations by teachers and auditory responses by learners.

Color-Coded Maps Promote Visual Recognition

When using Thinking Maps as an instructional approach, particularly with young children (Pre-K–2) and children with developmental delays or disabilities, we recommend using drawings, pictures, photos, actual objects, or models as much as possible to further enhance and reinforce children's ability to associate and connect visually and auditorily (see and hear) the concepts, ideas, and relationships described and discussed using the different TMaps. Matching written words with pictures, objects, or models is a well-accepted high-quality language strategy that provides learners with rich language-literacy connections (including phonological and phonemic awareness, phonics, and word recognition) that is particularly beneficial to both emergent and struggling readers.

It is equally helpful to color-code the maps, especially when first introducing and modeling the TMaps with young children in preschool and kindergarten as well as with children with disabilities and Dual Language Learners. While we agree that children use all modalities to learn, TMaps clearly emphasize the visual modality first and foremost

as the dominant modality through which learners perceive and interpret most information (Hyerle, 2009). Primary (red, blue, and yellow) and secondary (orange, green, and purple) colors are one of the earliest concepts that young children can visually recognize and name. Color-coding the maps with consistency helps children to readily recognize, name, and apply the correct thought process with each map (as captured in the chapter-opening vignette).

While Thinking Maps Inc. uses only white backgrounds for all commercially produced TMaps, there are clear benefits to consistently using a specific primary or secondary color with each map, helping young children to recognize and understand each thinking pattern. Black lines and print on colored backgrounds are easier for young emergent readers and writers, who are still developing their visual discrimination, to visually process in contrast to white backgrounds. Generally, we recommend the following coding system:

- Circle Map—Red
- Bubble Map—Yellow
- Double-Bubble Map—Orange
- Brace Map—Blue
- Tree Map—Green
- Flow Map—Purple
- Bridge Map—Pink
- Multi-Flow Map—White

Color coding can be particularly helpful for young children who have not yet developed beyond centration, in which their focused attention is generally limited to one characteristic or dimension of the learning experience. A color-code system provides another visual cue that children can easily identify and learn to associate with the corresponding map and cognitive process in order to efficiently use and organize new information.

The Frame of Reference

At any time and with every map, learners may additionally draw a rectangular frame around a map either with guidance from the teacher or independently. This represents one's Frame of Reference, or metacognitive frame. For example, a high school student may have sketched out a Flow Map and identified half a dozen turning points in the flow of a novel. By drawing the frame around the map, learners can jot down what influenced this analysis and the references in the text. Emergent readers and writers can dictate their frames of reference to an adult or older child.

The framing tool goes beyond merely referencing *what* one knows in order to ask the learners *how* they know the information within each map. Thinking Maps Inc. recommends the use of a color-code system to help learners differentiate the three frames of reference:

- Source Frame—Green Print
- Influencing Frame—Blue Print
- Reflective Frame—Red Print

The different frames of reference are designed to help children mindfully think about the three key points of reference for the information that they currently know and understand. Together, the three frames of reference represent a culturally sensitive and responsive practice by valuing what individual learners know and understand. The Source Frame (using green print) is in reference to the child's background knowledge and prior experiences. This frame helps the child to identify the "origin" from which the child has meaningfully constructed and used the information in purposeful ways.

The Influencing Frame (using blue print) helps the child to identify whether the concepts or ideas that they include in their map represent a point of view or perspective shared by an individual (such as a teacher or classmate) or a group (such as their family). An influential Frame of Reference often taps into social, cultural, regional, racial, and ethnic aspects that can influence a child's way of knowing, understanding, and expressing different topics, ideas, and concepts. Often referred to as "funds of knowledge," this framework holds particular relevance to diverse learners and will be discussed in greater detail in Chapter 5.

Finally, the Reflective Frame (using red print) challenges children to identify the main idea and to explain why it is important. This encourages children to concentrate on the overarching concept or central idea. As a higher-order critical thinking skill, children must learn to focus on the idea that matters most without distraction by the supporting details (attention-focusing using inhibitory control). This Frame of Reference holds particular relevance in helping to promote reading and writing comprehension as young children, for example, summarize and retell stories read in class.

Over time, children learn to recognize the significance of the different frames. This gained knowledge further guides and supports their ability to effectively apply each Frame of Reference as they learn and construct new content, ideas, and concepts.

It is equally helpful to create and use three versions of the Thinking Maps across three learning arrangements with young children: (1) Large Whole-Group Circle Time Maps, (2) Small-Group or Pair-Share Maps, and (3) Individual Maps. To make the whole-group maps, purchase solid-colored vinyl tablecloths at party or discount stores and draw the map diagram on the corresponding tablecloth using a bold black permanent marker (Figure 1.4).

For small-group maps, purchase inexpensive vinyl placemats or laminate large colored construction or poster paper with the map diagrams written in bold black permanent marker (Figure 1.5). Finally, the individual maps can be formatted onto construction paper, colored printer sheets, or colored plastic overlays (Figure 1.6). After children have experienced the eight TMaps in a variety of cooperative learning arrangements, they will be able to create and use each map diagram independently.

Since the mid-1990s, Thinking Maps Inc. has offered a set of eight very large, laminated, dry-erase "cooperative desk maps" (display both sides) for facilitating cooperative learning and for teacher use for small-group and whole-classroom use, developed by David Hyerle. On the back of each of the eight laminated surfaces is a "starter pattern" that shows a graphic primitive for each respective TMap (with a Frame of Reference) for students and/or teachers to generate a more fully developed map based on the content learning task. On the reverse side of each Desk Map is an open space for users to create multiple TMaps together on the same erasable workspace. Around the perimeter of the open space is a visual reference and vocabulary for each of the eight TMaps.

This Cooperative Desk TMap set is easily used when teachers organize their classroom into eight

Figure 1.4. Large Plastic Tablecloth Maps

Figure 1.5. Small Individual Vinyl Place Mat Maps

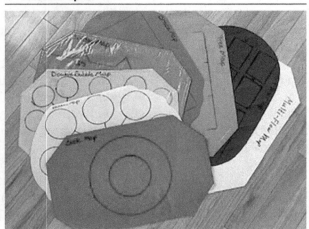

Figure 1.6. Colored Plastic Overlays

groups of learners, each with a specific focus or with the open-ended use of all of the TMaps. A range of colored pens for different groups may be used so that each TMap drawn by the group has a distinctive color and design. In addition, in the introductory training manual (*Thinking Maps: A Language for Learning*; Hyerle and Yeager, 2018) teachers are provided with a poster of each TMap to place in front of the classroom as a reference (just as teachers show the letters of the alphabet with pictures) so that learners are constantly reminded that these thinking processes as TMaps are for their use on a regular basis.

Questioning and Dialoguing Promote Auditory Skill Development

Children's language development and literacy development are central to each other. Language skills (expressive and receptive) rely heavily on the auditory learning channel and build gradually in a developmental progression over time as children expand their vocabulary, average sentence length, complexity and sophistication of sentence structure and grammar, and ability to express new ideas through words (Kipping et al., 2012). All young children require active engagement and ongoing practice across the four domains of language and literacy—speaking, listening, reading, and writing (National Association for the Education of Young Children [NAEYC], 2012). We suggest using mapping to address all of these simultaneously!

Quality interactions (like those encouraged and supported by Thinking Maps) help young children build their language skills and conceptual knowledge base (Dickinson & Porche, 2011; Lesaux & Kieffer, 2010; Nagy & Townsend, 2012). The more extensive a child's speaking and listening vocabulary, the greater the breadth and depth of words children can match to printed words.

Preschool vocabulary plays a critical role in later literacy development as it has been shown to correlate with reading comprehension levels in 4th grade (Dickinson & Porche, 2011). Yet, research indicates that substantial variation exists in the quality of teacher talk in early childhood classrooms (Bowers & Vasilyeva, 2011; Gámez & Levine, 2013; Greenwood et al., 2011) as well as in the quality of language used in the home (Isaacs, 2012). Duke and Block (2012) further note that vocabulary, reading comprehension, and conceptual and content knowledge are not adequately emphasized in many primary grade classrooms.

As elaborately discussed and demonstrated throughout this book, Thinking Maps provide a critical means to assist with stimulating, enhancing, and enriching young children's vocabulary, usage, and comprehension while expanding conceptual and content knowledge. TMaps encourage children to actively and strategically engage problem-solving strategies and skills involved in higher-order critical thinking. As detailed in the second edition of *Thinking Maps®: A Language for Learning* teachers' manual (Hyerle &

Yeager, 2018), guiding questions have been formulated to help teachers structure the conversation and discussion with each specific map. For example, the guiding questions cited in the teachers' guide (p. 25) for constructing a Circle Map are as follows:

- What do you know (or would like to know) about this word, topic, or idea?
- How would you define this idea?
- What information would you include in your brainstorming or defining this word, topic, or idea?
- What do you think this word, topic, or idea means?

Key words used by teachers to help facilitate the brainstorming process and considerations include context, list, define, brainstorm, identify, discuss, and generate. Additional questions used to create a Frame of Reference that encourages children to further reflect, contemplate, explain, and justify selected information include the following:

- How do you know this definition?
- Where are you getting your information?
- What sources did you reference to gather your information?
- Is there a specific point of view that is influencing your definition or ideas?
- What have you learned from this brainstorming process?
- Why is this information important?

A guiding question format and Frame of Reference is provided for all eight TMaps in the teachers' guide. Another example is the guiding question format cited in the teachers' guide (p. 61) for constructing a Multi-Flow Map, as follows:

- What are the causes and effects of this event?
- Why did this event take place?
- What will be the results of this event?
- What happened because of this event?
- What are the effects of this event?
- What was the motivation behind this event?

Key words used by teachers to help facilitate the cause-and-effect relationship and considerations include causes and effects, consequences, if/then, predict, motives, why, results, outcomes, and benefits. Additional questions used to create a Frame of Reference while using Multi-Flow Maps include the following:

- How do you know what you know about the causes and effects of this event?
- What source(s) did you use to identify the causes and effects?
- What could be influencing how you are thinking about these causes and effects?
- Did a specific time period influence the causes and effects?
- What do you now understand about the causes and effects of this event?
- Why is knowing about this event important?

In the case of the Circle Map about mice above, after completing the initial map, the book *Everyone Poops* is read and discussed. Additional information gleaned from the book can then be added and the book becomes the "Frame of Reference" (Figure 1.7).

The new information can be printed using another colored ink to easily designate the additional facts and source. The new information learned from the book can also be further analyzed, interpreted, and then applied to additional maps such as the Multi-Flow Map used to demonstrate cause-and-effect

Figure 1.7. Bubble Map: Describing Mice With a Frame of Reference Added

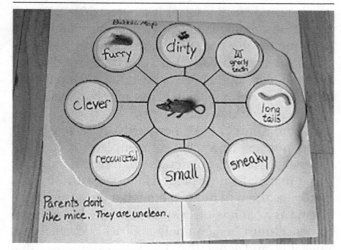

Figure 1.8. Multi-Flow Map: Cause–Effect Outcomes of Undigested Nutrients for Animals and Plant Life

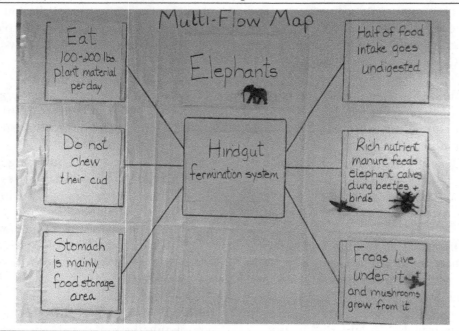

consequences for undigested nutrients elephants eat on animals and plant life (Figure 1.8).

Tactile Materials and Activities Increase Engagement

Young children rely heavily on their eyes, bodies, and hands to learn during sensorimotor development, as theorized by Piaget and likewise recognized and appreciated by Montessori and Froebel. Effective learning materials (or manipulatives) used during hands-on activities represent abstract concepts in concrete and tangible terms (Cameron, 2018). The effectiveness of the manipulative depends on how well it represents the concept to the learner. Classroom-based research in early logical-mathematical learning and development suggests that manipulatives help young children learn about number, space, and quantity (Guarino et al., 2013).

From Kohn's (2005) perspective, effective learning is not just active but also interactive. It is not enough to provide materials that are "hands-on"; these materials must pique children's curiosity and challenge them to think about what they are experiencing as a "minds-on" experience. The learning experience must be genuinely and richly challenging, engaging, and generative. Learning experiences that

are richly challenging include concepts and ideas that children find intriguing and interesting—a central tenet to the Project Approach as well.

Since the late 1980s, the mission of Smithsonian's Science Education Center has been to shift science education from the traditional didactic, teacher-centered learning to a more object-driven, child-centered approach to learning. With over 154 million objects in the collection, the center has developed units around the objects (e.g., rocks and minerals), bringing objects into classrooms, and getting learners to actively engage with them. TMaps help learners to actively integrate visual graphic representations of cognitive processes with linguistic auditory-processing within cooperative learning arrangements.

The use of dry-erase cooperative desk maps (noted above) and/or the creation of large and small vinyl maps combined with photos, pictures, concrete objects, or models (manipulatives) further enhance and strengthen the learning experience for young children as a multisensory approach by simultaneously tapping into tactile (hands-on) and kinesthetic (movement) modalities (Counsell et al., 2017; Counsell & Peat, 2017). Just as children use visuo-motor, spatial, and language skills when they draw and write, they integrate these same skills as they place photos, pictures, objects, or models on maps to communicate what they know and understand about a topic or idea, as we saw earlier in the TMaps related to mice. Children with visual impairments or with fine motor delays who struggle to draw and write information on their maps can use yarn or chenille wires to more easily form the lines, circles, and boxes on their maps.

Learning and development of concepts and skills is not achieved in isolation but instead is interdependent. For this reason, no singular skill or activity causes all others to develop. Rather, development is a complex system that is "mutually embedded and interdependent" (Thelen, 2005, p. 259). As demonstrated by Thinking Maps, skills develop simultaneously in "co-development" as children's development of one skill contributes toward their development of other skills (Kim et al., 2018). Hence, TMaps provide an ideal context for integrating concepts and skill development efficiently and effectively for maximum learning outcomes. As we will discuss below, the mental operation or cognitive process of creating or understanding categories requires the interdependent processes of becoming aware of the context (Circle Map) identifying attributes (Bubble Map), comparing attributes between and among objects or ideas (Double-Bubble Map), and then inductively or deductively developing a hierarchical classification (Tree Map). This means that as children are constructing categories they are most often unconsciously drawing upon at least these other cognitive processes, if not others. Thinking Maps, over time, thus become natural visual scaffolds for building higher-order thinking from the ground up.

CONCLUSION

As described and detailed throughout this chapter, the use of Thinking Maps is much more than a pre-writing framework for learners of all ages. In fact, TMaps are both an important instructional approach for teachers and an equally powerful learning framework for learners. TMaps actively engage children cooperatively as they use the different cognitive processes to help them think, talk, see, reflect, learn, and "draw out" their emerging schemata about topics, ideas, and themes that are interesting and relevant to their lives across the content areas.

We hope to have further challenged you with specific recommendations designed to increase young children's active participation during TMap activities. Creating permanent but also adaptable TMaps that can be used over and over during whole- and small-group instruction together with a variety of manipulatives serve to bring the TMaps to life for young children. Tapping into their four learning modalities (visual, auditory, kinesthetic, tactile) simultaneously stimulates and supports children's executive function (EF) skills—working memory, cognitive flexibility, and inhibitory control. While increasing the "hands-on" aspect of TMaps is helpful and developmentally beneficial to young children, we must also remember that manipulatives alone are not a panacea. The use of tactile TMaps and manipulatives with young children are only as meaningful and purposeful as the ways in which we employ them mindfully and with thoughtful mediation as educators.

CHAPTER 2

Thinking Maps Across Developmental Domains

An impressive revelation was the focus of a story told by a teacher about two brothers doing homework. A kindergartener said to his middle school brother, "Oh, you're doing a Bubble Map. That's for describing." The older brother asked how he knew that. The younger brother informed him that he learned about that at school, surprising the older brother completely (Jackson, 2011, p. 60).

Child development domains and early learning have been discussed, framed, and organized using a variety of categories. Different fields and disciplines have used various categories to help guide and inform practice, research, and policy as it pertains to young children from birth to age 8 (IOM & NRC, 2015). As suggested by the Institute of Medicine (IOM) and National Research Council (NRC), the chosen categorizations are less relevant as long as they are cognizant and inclusive of all elements that contribute to child development and early learning. Regardless of the framework and categories used, it is imperative to remember that the different domains do not develop or operate in isolation but instead are equally "interactive and mutually reinforcing rather than hierarchical" (2015, p. 87). Consequently, development in one domain enables and mutually supports learning and development in other domains. It is for this reason that any assessment of learning and skill development often crosses and pertains to multiple domains.

DEVELOPMENTALLY APPROPRIATE PRACTICE

Developmentally Appropriate Practice (DAP) is commonly referenced and outwardly embraced as an accepted approach or framework for how to effectively develop and implement high-quality learning experiences with the full range of young children (0–8 years). In the current Position Statement, NAEYC (2012) defines "development" broadly to include all aspects that contribute to children's learning that include abilities, disabilities, social identities, cultural and familial experiences, interests, and languages— "all of which reflect deeply personal interpretations that children construct within specific social and cultural contexts" (p. 5).

The construct of "appropriate" is more allusive with implicit biases that generally reflect and reinforce the dominant culture's normative views. The need to overcome this tendency challenges early childhood educators, for whom the vast majority (White females) represent the dominant culture, to learn to understand and recognize practice that is truly "appropriate" developmentally for any given child as determined from the individual child's vantage point.

Intentional decision making used to promote optimal learning and developmental outcomes seems to be a straightforward proposition that most (if not all) educators proclaim as the overarching goal for their daily instruction. Whether the actual practices selected and used regularly by educators are "developmentally appropriate" too often goes unchallenged and is never called into question because it is familiar and comfortable.

As described in this chapter and throughout this book, Thinking Maps are used intentionally in developmentally appropriate ways to promote young children's metacognition, to improve teaching practice, and to increase learning outcomes for children across developmental domains and academic content areas. The organizational framework adopted by the authors to explain and illustrate the learning and developmental benefits of TMaps identifies four key interacting and overlapping domains: (1) cognitive development, (2) socioemotional development, (3) physical development and health, and (4) general learning competencies (IOM & NRC, 2015). According to this framework, teaching and learning with TMaps has the greatest potential to positively impact children's cognitive and socioemotional development in addition to general learning competencies (see Table 2.1).

In contrast to the traditional application of Thinking (process) Maps, graphic organizers, and brainstorm webs as pre-writing activities, TMaps with young children are used throughout the teaching–learning process. Beyond the classroom and Pre-K–12 use of TMaps, the ultimate goal of the use of this model is for all learners to have agency in developing these fundamental, interrelated cognitive processes that are evolving throughout one's life. Actually, few learners of any age have a conscious awareness of how these fundamental processes of mind and brain drive their everyday thinking, learning problem solving, and decision making.

The use of tactile maps and concrete materials help to improve the developmental appropriateness of the TMaps and related metacognitive processes across a broad range of development, learning, and experience for children 3 to 8 years of age. Opportunities for children to complete individual maps further empower and encourage children to fully utilize their identity, voice, and agency in ways that are culturally responsive and sensitive to diverse strengths, needs, experiences, and perspectives. The goal for Thinking Maps is not to standardize teaching (and learning) into a one-size-fits-all box.

As illustrated by the chapter-opening vignette, very young children can learn to readily recognize

Table 2.1. Domains of Child Development and Early Learning

Developmental and Learning Domain	General Components
Cognitive Development	• Cognitive Skills and Concept Knowledge shared across subjects and distinct to specific subjects
Socioemotional Development	• Emotion/Regulation • Relational Security • Capacities for Empathy and Relatedness • Socioemotional Well-Being • Mental Health
Physical Development and Health	• Safety • Nutrition • Growth • Sensory and Motor Development • Fitness
General Learning Competencies (Approaches to Learning or Intellectual Habits)	• General Cognitive Skills • Attention • Memory • Cognitive Self-Regulation • Executive Function • Reasoning • Problem Solving • Learning Skills and Dispositions • Initiative • Curiosity • Motivation • Engagement • Persistence

Sources: IOM and NRC (2015). *Transforming the workforce for children birth through age 8: A unifying foundation.* Washington, DC: The National Academies Press.

and apply various TMaps to guide and support their understanding. Clearly, Thinking Maps can most directly promote general learning experiences as a whole, and indirectly impact physical and healthy growth and development to a lesser extent.

DOMAIN 1—COGNITIVE DEVELOPMENT

Children are born with active and inquisitive minds capable of insightful and complex thought. In the earliest years of life, foundations are established for sophisticated forms of learning, including later academic success. A child's growing capacities (or incapacities) for learning, complex thought, and supportive, empathetic relationships with others are shaped by remarkable developmental events happening within the growing brain.

These same capacities dramatically influence life chances and outcomes in relation to success, productivity, and satisfaction. Possible life paths are set in motion by early brain development that relies on bidirectional interactions between human biology and social and educational environments. The quality of interactions experienced by young children in early care, teaching, and learning environments provided by families and communities over time help to co-determine developmental, educational, biological, and health outcomes that characterize individual lives.

In recent decades, the most compelling developmental biology research has been the discovery of molecular, epigenetic processes by which environmental conditions have been shown to regulate the activation or deactivation of genes (Lam et al., 2012; Rutter, 2012). Human learning capacity is clearly grounded in brain development and brain circuitry. As explained by IOM and NRC (2015), "Rather than a structure built from a static 'blueprint,' the brain architecture that underlies learning is developed through a continuous, dynamic, adaptive interaction between biology and environment that begins at conception and continues throughout life" (p. 77). As a result, children's early experiences (including supports and stressors) affect gene expression and brain development. Adaptations resulting from mutual "nature" and "nurture" interactions affect all developmental domains.

Adult Language Impacts on Cognitive Development

Early cognitive development studies reveal that the young, developing mind is quite competent, active, and insightful from an early age, uniting disparate observations or discrete facts into coherent systems (Carey, 2009; Gopnik & Wellman, 2012). By the preschool years, children become quite astute in distinguishing adult speakers who will most likely provide reliable information from less reliable sources (Harris, 2012; Koenig & Doebel, 2013).

Epigenetic research demonstrates that experiences can alter gene expression, and as a result, high-quality, early learning experiences are critical. Rather than think about "nature" and "nurture" as an "either/or" relationship, epigenetics indicates that the biological and the environmental are intertwined and mutually interacting. Recognized as a pattern detector, the brain makes sense of the world by constructing patterns from the world, and from this vantage patterning becomes the entry point that helps connect brain functioning with visual tools (Hyerle, 2000). Therefore, early learning experiences within nurturing environments using TMaps can help promote possible gene expression and subsequent learning that positively affects all domains of human development.

It is therefore imperative that adults who work closely with young children understand and appreciate how their language impacts young children's cognitive growth and learning in many powerful and subtle ways. Educators, caregivers, and parents need to be fully aware of the benefits and pitfalls of the language they use as they interact with children. According to research, there are substantial variations in the quality of teacher talk in early childhood classrooms (Bowers & Vasilyeva 2011; Gámez & Levine 2013; Greenwood et al., 2011) as well as the quality of language used in the home (Isaacs 2012). Evidence further suggests that poverty and discrimination combined with poor-quality health care and education can lead to challenges that can impact the home language environment and children's development (Perkins et al., 2013). Parents not only support vocabulary acquisition by boosting children's exposure to words, parent–child interactions also offer a uniquely powerful context for intergenerational transmission of attitudes, beliefs, and knowledge (Thompson, 2006). It then becomes imperative that parents and educators develop and use maximally effective strategies to help facilitate young children's acquisition of new vocabulary (Bauer et al., 2016).

The development of best practices depends largely on increasing our understanding of early differences in vocabulary acquisition. A study by Shavlik and colleagues (2020) found that vocabulary gaps among young children are not characterized solely by accumulated vocabulary alone, but rather by the skills and strategies available to children for building vocabulary. We believe that TMaps can help children develop critically needed metacognitive skills and strategies used to promote vocabulary development.

Social interactions focused on child-directed language during shared activities such as dramatic play, snack time, board games, or class meetings are cognitively provocative as they invoke children's interest and attention within high-quality, language-rich learning environments (Jacoby & Lesaux, 2014). Embedding cognitive stimulation into social interaction creates an emotional context that elicits children's curiosity while enabling them to focus their thinking on new discoveries (IOM & NRC, 2015).

Engaging young children in daily talk is essential in developing their minds, playing a key role in helping them to construct knowledge of their surrounding world and the concepts and ideas they encounter—conceptual knowledge that forms the cornerstone of later reading success (IOM & NRC, 2015). The eight Thinking Maps provide caregivers and educators an important framework and model for how to encourage and support children's ability to visualize and express their higher-order complex ideas, concepts, and advanced vocabulary.

Cognitive Development and Thinking Maps

As active observers, young children build explanatory systems based on implicit theories used to organize their knowledge with causal principles and causal relations that enable them to predict, explain, and reason about relevant phenomena. These implicit theories help infants and toddlers to understand and make sense of how the world of people, living things, objects, and numbers operate. As young children develop their own intuitive "map" of mental processes (Baillargeon et al., 2009; Saxe, 2013), they transform how they respond to people and what they learn from them in a spiraling, circular fashion.

Children's implicit theories have equally important implications for teaching and learning. For example, failure to consider children's developing theories can lead educators to oversimplify materials designed for children. For example, if educators assume that young children are only "concrete" thinkers who cannot reason abstractly, then the tendency is to focus on descriptive activities without opportunities to advance their conceptual frameworks.

Preschoolers are intuitive and experiential learners who tend to figure things out by "doing" rather than using quiet "mental" contemplation. Yet, the tendency by educators to underestimate preschoolers' and kindergartners' cognitive abilities is a persistent issue and concern, for which the negative impact is greatest for children with fewer prior learning experiences (Clements & Sarama, 2014).

One kindergarten study by Claessens, Engel, and Curran (2014) found that, when assessed, children's actual performance was six to eight times what was estimated by their own teachers and other experts in consulting, teacher education, and educational research. Furthermore, this same study determined that kindergarten teachers spent the majority of their instructional time teaching familiar, basic content that children had already mastered even though children benefited more with advanced reading and mathematics content. When teachers practice in ways that are cognizant of children's cognitive progress, they directly and intentionally enlist and infuse children's existing knowledge and skills into new learning situations.

Metacognition refers to the process of drawing from various mental resources when learners face a dilemma or some type of obstacle; need to plan a course of action; monitor that strategy while executing it; and then reflect on the strategy in order to evaluate its productiveness in terms of the intended outcomes (Hyerle, 1996, 2009). With this in mind, Hyerle conceptualized and mindfully developed the eight TMaps to help learners of all ages "think about their thinking" by allowing their thoughts to become "visual." This book serves to make young children's experiences using TMaps even more tactile with the use of concrete maps and materials.

Elementary children's growing cognitive abilities enable them to pursue discoveries independently, using alternative inquiry strategies like TMaps with greater persistence in problem solving and determination to figure things out. As children engage with Thinking Maps, they use their cognitive regulation or, more precisely, Executive Functions (working memory, inhibitory control, and cognitive flexibility) to help organize their schema of understanding about any given topic, idea, or concept according to one or more of the eight cognitive processes (as detailed in Chapter 1). In summation, cognition encompasses the mental functions involved in attention, thinking, understanding, learning, remembering, solving problems, and making decisions that, combined, enable individuals to accomplish goals and negotiate the world (see Chapter 6).

For example, whales and sharks are two familiar animals that young children see depicted in children's literature, cartoons, animated movies, and documentaries. Since both animals live in oceans, children may have constructed a misconception that both animals are a type of fish. After reading literature, watching a documentary, or visiting a local science museum or aquarium with multiple opportunities to observe live specimens or examine and explore real-life artifacts (e.g., teeth, bones) related to oceanic life, children can complete two separate Circle Maps to brainstorm what they know or believe

Figure 2.1. Computer-Generated Circle Maps: Brainstorming About Whales and Sharks

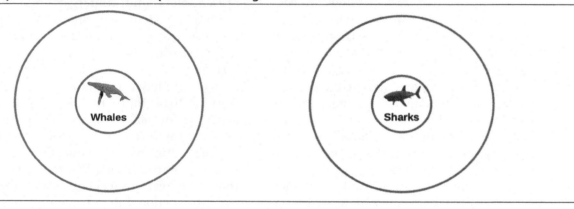

Figures 2.2 and 2.3. Circle Maps: Brainstorming About Whales and Sharks

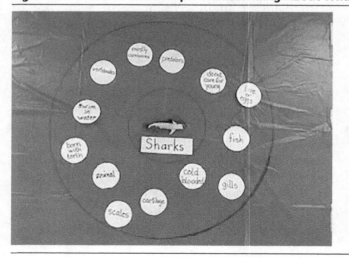
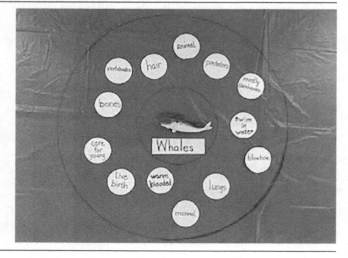

about whales on the first map and sharks on the second map (Figures 2.1–2.3).

In cooperative groups, preschool and primary grade teachers can guide and facilitate children's completion of a Double-Bubble Map to compare and contrast the similarities and differences (Figures 2.4 and 2.5). Children must use their working memory as they denote which facts apply to each animal.

Children in the primary grades use more complex vocabulary and grammar as they increase their ability to make mental representations, although they continue to rely on real-life references and materials such as the models, objects, and photos

recommended for use with TMaps. Advanced vocabulary and scientific terminology such as mammal, fish, lungs, gills, vertebrates, carnivores, predators, krill, plankton, cold-blooded, and warm-blooded used to compare and contrast whales and sharks in the Double-Bubble Map further deepen and expand children's schema of scientific knowledge and understanding.

Additional maps used to challenge and promote children's critical thinking about whales and sharks include Brace Maps to show the internal and external parts of whales and sharks; Flow Maps to sequence whale and shark life cycles or food

Figure 2.4. Computer-Generated Double-Bubble Map: Comparing/Contrasting Sharks and Whales

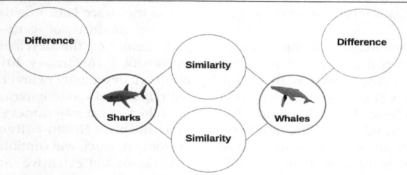

Figure 2.5. Double-Bubble Map: Comparing/Contrasting Sharks and Whales

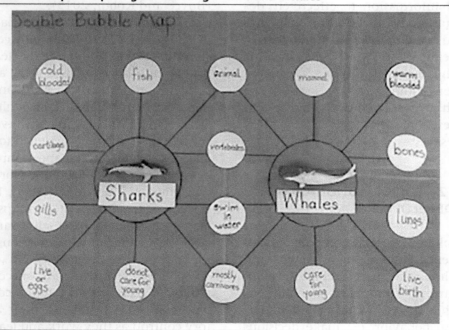

chains; Tree Maps to classify the different species of whales and sharks, or one Tree Map used to group and sort whale species and shark species or the five vertebrate animal groups (fish, amphibians, reptiles, birds, and mammals); and a Multi-Flow Map to depict how whales were historically hunted by humans for a variety of purposes (such as whale blubber or oil).

Centration is a familiar characteristic of preoperational children that causes them to focus on the most obvious aspects of what they perceive (such as size, color, or texture) but do not help to define or differentiate contrasting concepts. As children grow and learn, it is imperative that they have multiple and ongoing opportunities to use and develop their power of observation in order to learn to distinguish the defining characteristics from those that do not.

As children use Tree Maps to group and sort items into categories, they use their working memory to recall and use multiple facts as they map each item according to similarities and differences. As they denote the various facts, they must discern which facts matter, without being distracted by facts that are irrelevant, learning to stop or repress impulsive responses using inhibitory control. Children manage, organize, and apply the relevant facts (such as gills, lungs, and blowholes) analytically using their cognitive flexibility as they shift between pieces of information to effectively define, contrast, group, and sort different types into the two designated categories: whales and sharks. Instructional strategies (like TMaps) that encourage and promote higher-level thinking, creativity, and abstract understanding, as described above, are associated with greater cognitive achievement by children in preschool (Diamond et al., 2013) and primary grades.

DOMAIN 2—SOCIOEMOTIONAL DEVELOPMENT

As a complex, multidimensional construct, socioemotional competence is increasingly viewed and appreciated as an important part of child development and early learning with critical contributions that enable the child to (1) manage and understand emotions and behavior, (2) make decisions and achieve goals, and (3) establish and maintain positive relationships, which includes showing and feeling empathy for others (Denham & Brown, 2010; Heckman et al., 2013; IOM & NRC, 2015). An emerging body of research reveals potential relationships between the dimensions of socioemotional competence with cognition, early learning, and later academic achievement (Bierman et al., 2008a, 2008b).

As described earlier in this chapter, epigenetic processes play a critically essential role in the successful emergence of social, educational, and biological capacities (IOM & NRC, 2015). New and promising research continues to produce evidence (e.g., Shonkoff & Garner, 2012) that multiple variations in human developmental and educational trajectories trace back origins in early childhood; are the products of gene–environment interplay (Center on the Developing Child at Harvard University, 2016; Meaney, 2010; Rutter, 2006); and influence developing neural circuits and processes with direct links to long-term health, disease, and life achievement trajectories (Fox et al., 2010; U.S. Department of Health & Human Services, 2016). Ongoing research will continue to demonstrate the remarkable and extensive interplay among social environments, genes, and epigenetic processes in ways that genetic and environmental variations converge in typical and atypical development (Boyce and Kobor, 2015).

Human beings are largely social beings who compulsively crave contact and engagement with others (Hyerle, 1996, 2009). Early learning, discussed throughout this book, is a social activity largely dependent on responsive, serve-and-return interactions between children and adults (Center on the Developing Child at Harvard University, 2021). One conceptual framework designed to encompass social and emotional learning and competencies has been developed by the Collaborative for Academic, Social, and Emotional Learning (2015). It is organized according to five interrelated groups of competencies: (1) self-management, (2) self-awareness, (3) responsible decision making, (4) relationship skills, and (5) social awareness (see IOM & NRC, 2015).

Children's capacities to successfully engage in academic tasks and to interact constructively with teachers while sustaining their attention (inhibitory control) as they work and learn collaboratively with agemates relies heavily on these areas of social competence (Denham & Brown, 2010). TMaps adaptability to a wide range of learning group arrangements make it an ideal approach to help educators optimize social contexts for learning. In Chapter 4, the authors elaborate extensively on how TMaps can be used systematically to promote children's social-emotional development during cooperative learning arrangements within inclusive, democratic learning communities.

DOMAIN 3—PHYSICAL AND HEALTHY

Overall, health plays a major role and has a significant influence on children's early learning and academic achievement. It is a widely accepted tenet in early childhood that healthy children are better prepared to learn, just as children's participation in high-quality early childhood programs leads to better health outcomes as adults, which likewise contributes toward intergenerational well-being. Nutritional, high-quality dietary intake is critical to children's health, development, and learning. While the influence of health on learning is important, the connection between physical and cognitive development has greater relevance as it pertains to Thinking Maps—thus, more attention will be devoted to this symbiotic relationship.

For young children, cognitive and physical development go hand in hand as growth in one domain positively impacts growth in the other. Part of healthy physical development is healthy fine and gross motor development. This entails sensory development (including visual and auditory) to which TMaps is particularly beneficial, as described in Chapter 1, and musculoskeletal gross large motor as well as precisely controlled fine motor and oral motor skills such as speech production (Grissmer et al., 2010a; Pagani & Messier, 2012).

Recent studies have demonstrated strong links between fine motor skills and later academic achievement due to the same neural brain infrastructure controlling motor and cognition during learning that now calls for a shift in curricula that includes an increased focus on fine motor skills used in the arts (such as the visual arts, music, and dance), physical education, and play (Grissmer et al., 2010a, 2010b). As a model for teaching and learning, TMaps hold

particular promise in helping to support children's fine, sensory, and perceptual motor development.

Chapter 1 provided multiple examples and details of how to create and use the eight tangible plastic or vinyl TMaps to help young children visually organize, verbally discuss, and physically manipulate concepts and ideas. Using their fine motor skills, children manipulate actual objects, models, replicas, photos, and illustrated pictures related to the concepts and mental relationships across the different content areas on the different TMaps.

Children can also complete TMaps in cooperative small groups, pair shares, or independently using tag board, construction paper, or colored printer paper. They can use a variety of materials such as arts and craft materials to represent the concepts and ideas they place on their maps. The possibilities of materials and ways in which children choose to convey concepts, ideas, and relationships are virtually limitless.

DOMAIN 4—GENERAL LEARNING COMPETENCIES

General learning competencies have been labeled and categorized in a variety of ways. Executive function (the supervisory functions) that regulate and control cognitive activity (cognitive regulation) impacting learning enable children to persevere with tasks, including learning tasks, despite fatigue, distraction, or lack of motivation (Vitiello et al., 2011). These skills are often conceptualized in preschool as the quality of how children approach learning or "noncognitive skills" that include learning competencies such as self-control, persistence, self-discipline, motivation, and self-esteem (Heckman, 2007). Noncognitive skills not only support learning and achievement but are also highly relevant to cognitive skills in such areas as language, mathematics, science, and other traditional academic fields (Cunha & Heckman, 2010).

TMap activities provide learners with ample opportunities to develop executive functions and children's noncognitive approaches to learning. The level of engagement with Thinking Maps, regardless of the grouping arrangement, support children's overall perseverance. This is due in large part to children's desire to participate in tangible TMap activities that help to diminish the fatigue, distraction, or decreased motivation that children otherwise experience during more direct-teach, skill-drill instruction.

Regular and ongoing opportunities to work with Thinking Maps can increase children's persistence, self-discipline, and self-control as they learn to take turns sharing ideas and materials as they explore and learn about different topics, ideas, and concepts. Over time, learners working with TMaps become confident in their ability to organize and demonstrate what they know and understand about a chosen topic. This in turn increases their self-esteem as capable and competent learners (and communicators) and thus further inspires and motivates them to want to learn and share more.

CONCLUSION

This chapter highlighted the important scientific research around epigenetics, its critical role in early brain development, and the importance of providing high-quality early learning experiences like Thinking Maps to promote children's development across the developmental domains. When used

effectively within socially dynamic learning communities, TMaps can help maximize children's brain development as they actively (1) engage their cognition using the eight mental processes and executive functions; (2) use expressive and receptive language skills to share and respond to each other's thoughts and ideas; and (3) develop social-emotional competence as they manage their emotional responses and behavior toward others in order to maintain positive relationships within cooperative group arrangements.

The extent to which Thinking Maps directly support physical development and health specifically are limited to a lesser extent in contrast to other domains. The use of tangible maps and materials provide important opportunities for children to practice their fine motor skills, manual dexterity, and eye–hand coordination as they use their visual–spatial orientation to create maps, place items on TMaps, and use a variety of writing tools to complete map activities. The flexibility of Thinking Maps makes them readily available and easily adaptable as a teaching and learning framework across developmental domains and the different content areas, as discussed in detail in Chapter 3.

Thinking Maps Across Academic Content Areas

As a Pre-K teacher, I find Thinking Maps to be an effective and powerful instructional tool for the teacher as well as a meaningful and practical learning and organizational tool for the student. I like using various maps to introduce topics, such as an amphibian unit on frogs in which a Circle Map is used to present new information; a Flow Map displays the life cycle and metamorphosis; and a Double-Bubble Map compares frogs with toads. Together, these strategies become the critical component of an effective learning experience. (S. Counsell, personal communication, February 15, 2000)

The American Institutes for Research report *Does Deeper Learning Improve Student Outcomes?* suggests that important 21st-century skills can best be achieved through "deeper learning" (Bitter & Loney, 2015). In order to achieve deeper learning, teachers must help children develop (1) a deeper understanding of core academic content, (2) an ability to apply that understanding to novel problems and situations, and (3) a range of competencies, including people skills and self-control. As discussed in previous chapters, Thinking Maps help children to think deeply about core academic content using a range of processing skills with a variety of cooperative learning arrangements while fully utilizing their self-regulation and inhibitory control. Science, technology, engineering, and math content provide children with many opportunities to experience and solve novel problems and situations specifically using TMaps that will be explored in detail in this chapter.

The six dimensions of deeper learning (Chow, 2010; Trilling, 2010; William and Flora Hewlett Foundation, 2013) are as follows:

1. Mastery of core academic content
2. Critical thinking and problem solving
3. Effective communication
4. Ability to work collaboratively
5. Learning how to learn
6. Academic mindsets

These dimensions are a central focus of national K–12 initiatives that can be actively employed by learners during TMap activities. While many approaches, strategies, and tools are used to support academic learning, critical thinking, problem solving, communicating, and collaborating throughout the teaching–learning process, few models emphasize "how to learn" and develop "academic mindsets" like Thinking Maps. Unlike other models, TMaps actively engage learners in how to use the eight metacognitive processes to learn and understand academic content as well as the academic mindsets of how to think like a scientist, mathematician, artist, writer, and engineer.

Young children's acquisition of content knowledge and competencies fundamental to later academic success rely on these 21st-century interrelated skills and abilities that are used within and across disciplines. In developmental science, time as a factor is a recurrent theme playing a central role in developmental outcomes. Across the life span, how experience affects learning and development changes dynamically as critical and sensitive periods open and close. During sensitive periods (windows of early life when plasticity is highly dependent on experience), the brain is especially responsive to experiences and exposures, resulting in irreversible changes in brain circuitry (Fox et al., 2010; Takesian & Hensch, 2013). Research now shows that, over time, the brain's plasticity is initiated and constrained by molecular "triggers" and "brakes" (Takesian & Hensch, 2013), further demonstrating that the onset and offset of critical periods are due to epigenetic molecular mechanisms (Fagiolini et al., 2009).

> Designing effective materials in a given domain or subject matter requires knowing what implicit theories children hold, what core causal principles they use, and what misconceptions and gaps in knowledge they have, and then using empirically validated steps to help lead them to a more accurate, more advanced conceptual framework. (IOM & NRC, 2015, p. 92)

As noted by Jackson (2011), "thinking processes are universal, and Thinking Maps help students transfer these cognitive skills across content areas and grade levels" (p. 60). As detailed in the Introduction, TMaps offer learners a consistent, flexible, and transferable visual language that is adaptive across life span learning. Still, materials used with young children are only as effective as the educator who integrates them into high-quality learning experiences.

THINKING MAPS INSPIRE TALKING, READING, AND WRITING

Children's language development and literacy development are interrelated, integral, reciprocal, and central to each other. Language skills build in a developmental progression over time as children increase their vocabulary, average sentence length, complexity and sophistication of sentence structure and grammar, and ability to express new ideas through words (Kipping et al., 2012). By attentively responding to children's questions, comments, actions, and emotions, adults promote children's expansion of word knowledge and relationships among them.

Learning and development rely heavily on stimulating environments with mutually respectful, reciprocal adult–child relationships (Wright et al., 2015). High-quality interactions help young children build their language skills and conceptual knowledge base that they will later use to read and understand complex text in high school, college, and career (Dickinson & Porche 2011; Lesaux & Kieffer 2010; Nagy & Townsend 2012). Furthermore, ongoing peer-to-peer interactions in classrooms have been found to positively impact children's vocabulary and expressive language abilities in much the same way as teacher interactions with children, especially when interacting peers have advanced language skills (Mashburn et. al., 2009). Eventual reading skill development depends in large part on children's oral language development (O'Connor et al., 2014).

Show-and-Tell Detectives Using TMaps

Show and Tell is a common and familiar oral language activity experienced during circle time meetings in many Pre-K–2 classrooms in the United States. During this language experience, children take turns bringing a special item to class that they want to share, describe, and often demonstrate its use to their friends in class.

One creative and innovative way to vary this language experience in ways that increase children's interest and engagement is to place the (mystery) item in a "feely" bag or box. Children take turns reaching into the container, describing what they are feeling (e.g., big, small, furry, soft, smooth, round, rectangular), and the teacher places the written adjectives on a Bubble Map. For example, a child brings a favorite toy, a stuffed ostrich, to place in the feely bag. Children then take turns describing what they feel (Figure 3.1).

The descriptive adjectives become clues to figure out and identify the item. Children's directed attention to identifying objects requires them to focus on relevant contexts and properties in order to accurately name it (Smith et al., 2010; Smith et al.,

Figure 3.1. Bubble Map: Describing a Mystery Item (Ostrich) in the Feely Bag

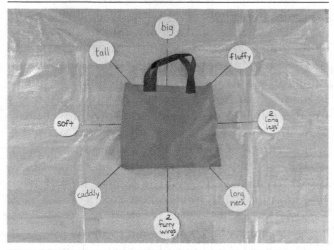

2002). As a learning–teaching activity, the "mystery item" facilitates inductive reasoning, as children use specific details or properties in order to formulate a generalized conclusion (in this case, naming the item). While many children may declare generally that the mystery item is a "stuffed animal" or a "bird," the challenge is to identify the specific type of stuffed animal or bird.

Once children have guessed and voted on what they think the item is, the child who owns the item takes it out and places it in the center of the Bubble Map. The child then confirms whether each chosen adjective accurately describes the item (e.g., two long legs, a long neck). Now that children can see the stuffed animal, additional adjectives can be included to more fully describe the stuffed animal, such as its color. Children may also add adjectives about ostriches based on what they have seen or heard, such as ostriches are fast, ostriches are shy, and so on (see Figure 3.2). If children disagree on whether ostriches are fast or slow, for example, this can inspire children to read books, conduct research on the internet, view videos, or visit zoos or petting farms to learn more about ostriches, allowing for enriched and dynamic discussions with terminology that further promotes scientific literacy development.

As noted by Booth (2009), young learners are particularly interested in conceptual information, and children are more likely to understand and retain information, including new vocabulary, when conceptual properties are specified. Tapping into children's interests helps to facilitate children's memory (Uncapher & Rugg, 2005). Increasing meaningful elaboration of concepts leads to more robust memories (Levin, 1988), which we argue can be promoted by TMaps.

Children can also ask questions to help them figure out what the mystery item can do or how it is used (e.g., "Do you play with it?" "Can you sleep with it?" "Can you eat it?"). The teacher writes each question and answer on a T-Chart (Figure 3.3). Research further demonstrates that adding this kind of causal information about artifacts (linking semantic information related to causes and effects together in meaningful ways) with questioning that directs attention to functionality can potentially enhance children's memory and word learning (Bauer et al., 2016; Booth, 2009). Hence, word extension

Figure 3.3. T-Chart—Mystery Item Questions and Answers

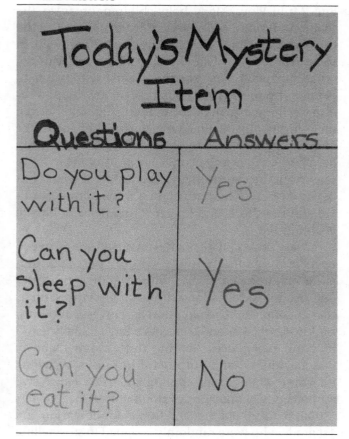

Figure 3.2. Bubble Map: Additional Adjectives Describing an Ostrich

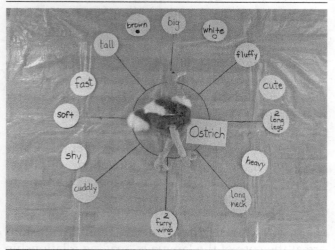

and development may be best supported when the ontological aspects (relations between concepts and categories) are emphasized in combination with young children's developing causal powers (Booth et al., 2005; Lavin & Hall, 2001).

Children use those additional clues inductively to try to identify the item by "function," capitalizing on children's particular sensitivity to, and interest in, and intrinsic motivation to use this type of information, as research evidence suggests (Alvarez & Booth, 2014; Booth, 2009; Greif et al., 2006; Kelemen et al., 2003). As children develop and become fluent with TMaps (often by 1st or 2nd grade), they can easily create their own Bubble Maps for generating descriptive language. In pairs and/or cooperative groups, children bring their individual ideas together, creating a synthesis TMap they present to the entire learning community.

Sharing Time With TMaps

Similar to Show and Tell, children like to take turns sharing life events and activities with others. Flow and Multi-Flow Maps help children organize the major and minor sequences of events as well as the causes and "ripple" effects of important moments in their lives, effectively and efficiently communicating what happened. For example, a child who wants to detail a trip to the park could use a Flow Map to sequence the playground equipment the child played on using photos or illustrated pictures of each type of equipment. A child who comes to school with a band-aid on her knee could use a Multi-Flow Map to explain the cause–effect relationship of what happened to her knee that resulted in needing a band-aid and the short- and longer-term effects of having been injured.

These kinds of dialogic conversations between peers and significant adults help to boost and integrate children's language with cognitive processes and overall socialization within safe, secure settings that encourage the exploration and investigation of a multitude of ideas and concepts related to daily activities and experiences. Sharing Time, as noted above, is a meaningful and purposeful form of storytelling for young children, promoting children's expressive and receptive language development. In fact, Gallets (2005) determined that children in kindergarten and 1st grade who were randomly assigned to storytelling

twice a week for 12 weeks made greater gains in vocabulary and recall than children assigned to story reading for the same duration. TMaps provide a visual scaffold, and when recorded as a TMap, become an important record of the child's verbal storytelling and working memory.

Thinking Maps Complement Interactive Storybook Reading

Interactive storybook reading between children and adults is one of the best-documented methods for improving children's vocabularies (O'Connor et al., 2014; Zucker et al., 2013) and literacy skills in general when combined with highly engaging children's books (Farrant & Zubrick, 2012; Sénéchal, 2010). Allowing time and space for book-centered conversations stimulates children's interests and introduces new words as children ask questions that may or may not be central to the story. As children encounter unfamiliar words during conversations, storytelling, and book reading, they link words to existing schema, further expanding their receptive language into their own conversations (expressive language). A preschool study by Zucker and colleagues (2013) determined that *intentional talk* by teachers during storybook reading had strong correlations to longer-lasting effect on children's language skills in comparison to the *frequency* of storybook reading with children.

Stronger oral language competencies not only help young children acquire new language skills at a faster rate (Dickinson and Porche, 2011) but also help children learn key literacy skills more quickly (Cooper et al., 2002). Young children's listening (receptive language) and speaking (expressive language) abilities have been shown to have long-term effects on children's reading and writing abilities in 3rd through 5th grade (Lee, 2011). Preschoolers with larger vocabularies may develop phonemic awareness and the alphabetic principle with greater ease simply because they have a greater repertoire of words to draw on and to explore similarities and differences (IOM & NRC, 2015). Phonemic awareness and understanding the alphabetic principle, in turn, contribute significantly toward learning to read in kindergarten and 1st grade.

Expressive (oral and written) language skills (i.e., vocabulary, syntax, listening comprehension) are at the core of the language–reading relationship

(IOM & NRC, 2015; NICHD Early Child Care Research Network, 2005). Strong speaking and listening vocabularies are advantageous to readers of all ages, providing them with a wider and more varied field of words that they can attempt to match to print when reading, supporting reading comprehension (Suggate et al., 2018). Despite the research, Duke and Block (2012) have noted that in primary grade classrooms, vocabulary, reading comprehension, and conceptual and content knowledge are *not adequately emphasized*.

As described in Chapters 1 and 2, Thinking Maps actively encourage language and literacy as children use the eight metacognitive processes for drawing out the patterns of their thinking and oral language, thus reinforcing, as Vygotsky offers, "thought and language." Children ask and answer questions across the content areas, promoting expressive and receptive language development as they speak, write, read, and listen.

As suggested in Chapter 1, TMaps such as a Circle Map can be used to brainstorm prior to reading, much like a K-W-L is used to help determine and connect children's prior experience, knowledge, and understanding with the topic at hand. After reading the story, children can use a Bubble Map to describe a central character, item, or setting in the story. A Double-Bubble Map can compare and contrast two or more characters, items, or settings in the book or even compare and contrast the book just read with a previous book on the same topic or different version of the story. A Flow Map can sequence the events of the story, and a Multi-Flow Map can help children to identify the beginning, middle, climax, and consequence/ending to the story. A Brace Map can be used to demonstrate the parts of a key physical object or place central to the plot. A Tree Map can help children draw out the main ideas, secondary themes, and details while also grouping and sorting characters or items, or can even classify the story read in relation to other stories such as fiction and nonfiction. Finally, a Bridge Map can be used to highlight analogies of the different characters or items in the story as well as developing grammar, syntax, and vocabulary.

TMaps, in essence, become both a visual scaffold for generating and drawing out specific cognitive patterns as well as offering guiding questions: How would you describe and compare these characters? What was the sequence of the story? What caused the main character to act in a certain way? What do you think is the main idea in the story? Are there any other ideas? Linking essential questions to cognitive patterns soon becomes a foundation for reading stories and reading across the disciplines.

Like many fairytales, *Goldilocks and the Three Bears* has important and relatable morals to the story around belongings, ownership, and accountability, with obvious cause–effect consequences for the choices and decisions that are made. Stories with causality (the functional revelations or explanations regarding the "why" and "how" of what happens) have been found to be particularly interesting and appealing to young children (Alvarez & Booth, 2014; Greif et al., 2006). The specific causality of what happens as Goldilocks explores the different bowls of porridge, chairs, and beds in the story captivates young children's interest and attention as they can readily make sense of the "how" and "why" her experience with each item varies.

Animals are also a familiar and favorite topic, and one of the most popular subjects in children's books (Marriott, 2002). Since children's surroundings are filled with a variety of wild and domesticated animals that they encounter daily, it is no wonder that children are drawn to books about animals with great intrigue (DeLoache et al., 2011).

Prior to reading the story in a preschool or kindergarten class, a teacher positions a large Circle Map at the center of the floor with the class sitting around it. She asks the class, "What do we call this map?" The children eagerly respond, "Circle Map!" She then asks, "What do we do with the Circle Map? Children answer, "Brainstorm!" She then places an item (e.g., a stuffed bear and bear cutouts) in the center circle and asks the children to identify it; children raise their hands to tell her something they know about bears (Figure 3.4). Children's ideas will vary widely depending on their prior knowledge and experiences (e.g., books read; visits to the zoo, circus, or national park; educational TV programs).

The teacher then tells the class that she is going to read a book about a family of bears and invites the children to guess the title of the book (*Goldilocks and the Three Bears*). Holding up and showing children the book cover, she asks, "Is this story fiction (make believe) or nonfiction (real-life)? How do you know?" Children respond, "Fiction, because

Figure 3.4. Circle Map—Brainstorming About Bears

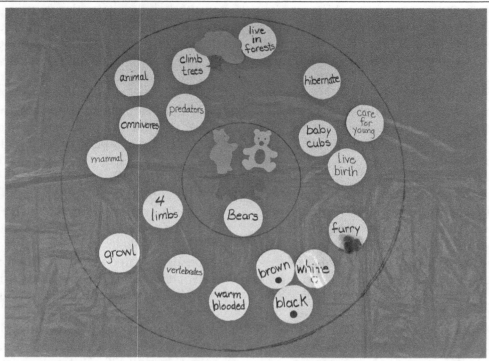

the bears are wearing clothes and live in a house. Real bears don't do that." Over the course of several days, the preschool class revisits the story and completes a different Thinking Map using one of the eight metacognitive processes (see Table 3.1).

Beyond what is presented here, there are clearly a multitude of applications that children can use in small groups, pairs, or independently to organize the ideas, concepts, and relationships in the story. Young children can readily relate to the two youngest fictional characters in the story: Goldilocks and Baby Bear. To help them think thoughtfully about these characters, they can complete a Bubble Map about one of the characters, such as Goldilocks (Figure 3.5) and then compare and contrast those characteristics with Baby Bear using a Double-Bubble Map (Figure 3.6).

Children describing Goldilocks as "naughty" or "bad" is based on her entering a house when no one is home and helping herself to their belongings. Young children can use a Flow Map to sequence the three types of each item that Goldilocks explores (Figure 3.7), and a Brace Map can be employed to break down the part–whole relationship

of the beds or chairs. Children can draw their own chair or cut out pictures of chairs from catalogs, sale flyers, or pictures printed off the internet to cut apart (Figure 3.8).

Children can further examine the relationships of the belongings that Goldilocks encountered as they group and sort (classify) the three bears' items using a Tree Map (Figure 3.9) and then reorganize the same information into analogies (such as Papa Bear's porridge is too hot) using a Bridge Map (Figure 3.10). The Tree Map application introduces young children to the mathematical concepts of seriation (e.g., small, medium, big bears) and double seriation (e.g., small bear–small bed), simultaneously promoting and supporting young children's logical-mathematical reasoning as well.

While it is very common for young children in the United States to eat cold cereal for breakfast, eating hot cereal or oatmeal, which is like porridge, may be less common today. A meaningful and relevant way to cap off this unit of study would be to discuss whether children have eaten oatmeal or porridge and whether they liked it. The class can enjoy a direct experience with porridge (using a crockpot),

Table 3.1. *Goldilocks and the Three Bears* **Metacognitive Analysis**

Goldilocks and the Three Bears

Thinking Map®	Metacognitive Process	Story Content
• Circle Map	• Brainstorm	• Bears
• Bubble Map	• Describe	• Goldilocks
• Double-Bubble Map	• Compare/Contrast	• Baby Bear and Goldilocks
• Flow Map	• Sequence	• Items Goldilocks Explores
• Brace Map	• Part/Whole	• Papa Bear's Chair
• Tree Map	• Group/Sort/Classify	• Each bear's belongings (e.g., Mama Bear's porridge, chair, and bed)
• Bridge Map	• Analogy	• Items and attributes (e.g., Papa Bear's porridge is too hot)
• Multi-Flow Map	• Cause–Effect	• Making porridge

Figure 3.5. Bubble Map—Describing Goldilocks

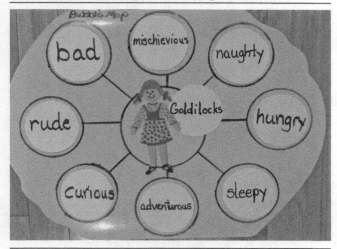

Figure 3.7. Flow Map: Sequencing Explored Belongings by Goldilocks

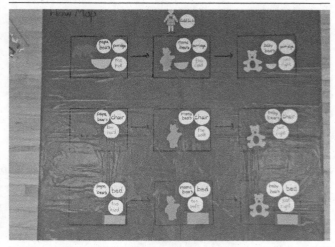

Figure 3.6. Double-Bubble Map—Comparing and Contrasting Goldilocks and Baby Bear

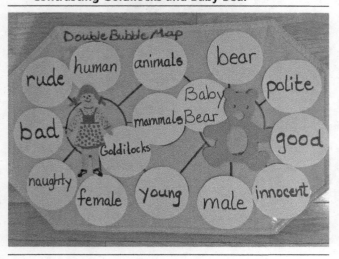

Figure 3.8. Brace Map: Part–Whole Relationship to Chairs

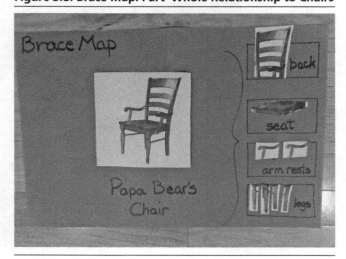

as they observe the causality of what happens when dry ingredients are combined with liquids (states of matter), stirred and heated together, and then eaten. Cooking activities like this generate meaningful causal mechanisms (mixing and heating) responsible

for a change in state that children can actively investigate and experience firsthand with close adult supervision. Children can record the instructions using a Multi-Flow Map (Figure 3.11).

In addition to honey, fruit, berries, cinnamon, or brown sugar can be provided (reflecting regional and cultural preferences) to help children sweeten the taste to their individual preference. Individual Multi-Flow Maps would then reflect each child's personal preferences.

To further illustrate the application of TMaps to support English Language Arts with young children, let's consider some possible book selections about wintertime. Prior to reading the first children's book, such as *Snowballs* by Lois Ehlert (1995), children can brainstorm everything they know about wintertime and place words, pictures, and winter items (such as mittens, a hat and scarf) on the large Circle Map (Figure 3.12).

Depending on where children live and the climate they experience, pictures, videos, and children's books can play an important role as "windows" into the lives and different outdoor activities experienced by people living in colder climates. Children's books,

Figure 3.9. Tree Map: Classifying the Three Bears' Belongings

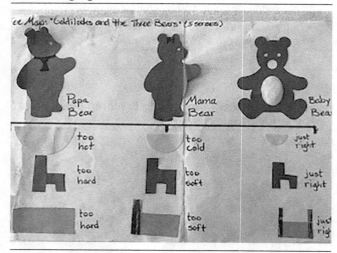

Figure 3.10. Bridge Map: Analogies of How Goldilocks Experienced Each Item

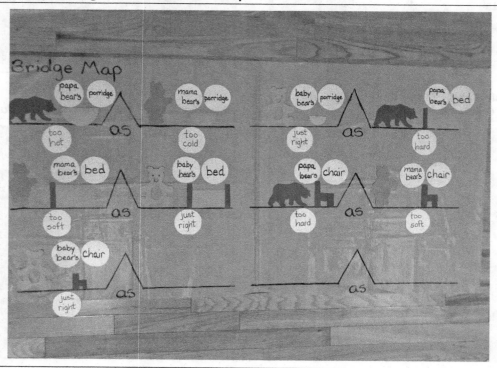

Figure 3.11. Multi-Flow Map: Cause–Effect Used to Make Porridge

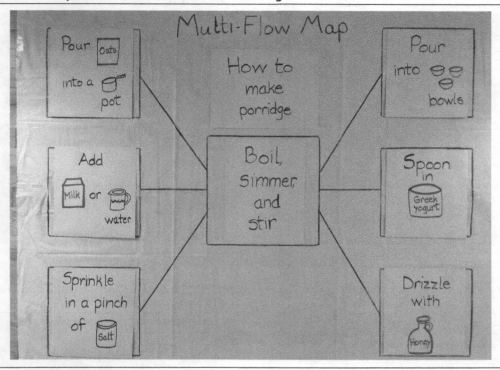

Figure 3.12. Circle Map: Brainstorming Wintertime With a Source Reference Frame

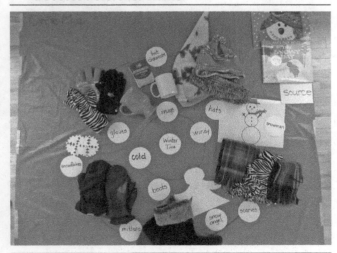

both fiction and nonfiction, are a critically important source of information and can be included as a Reference Frame on the TMap.

After reading the story, children can complete the different Thinking Maps to help them think deeply and mindfully about the story elements and main ideas, whether in whole group, cooperative small groups, in pairs, or individually. Teachers can also model for students how to use the metacognitive frame (of reference) around each of the TMaps and support reflection on how students' own lives are influencing how they are interpreting the story. There is no exact order in which to use maps to discuss and review the information presented in a story. Rather, maps can be used as needed to draw attention to and emphasize specific concepts, ideas, and facts as visual patterns of thinking that link together.

A Bubble Map can be used to describe a snowman, using adjectives such as cold, white, round, and smooth, whereas a Brace Map can break a snowman down into the different sections and parts (Figures 3.13 and 3.14). A Flow Map can be used to sequence the story events, such as the different snowpeople and pets introduced in the story or the sequence for building a snowman (Figure 3.15). Children can use a Bridge Map to draw analogies based on attributes such as the sun (feels) hot, as the snow (feels) cold (causal relationships) or language skills specific to grammar, vocabulary, and

Figure 3.13. Bubble Map: Describing a Snowman

Figure 3.14. Brace Map: Parts of a Snowman

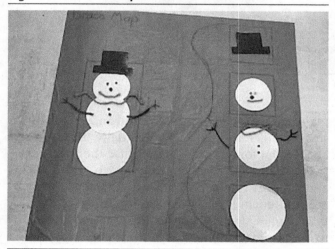

Figure 3.15. Flow Map: Sequencing Snowman Construction

Figure 3.16. Bridge Map: Singular and Plural Winter Item Analogies

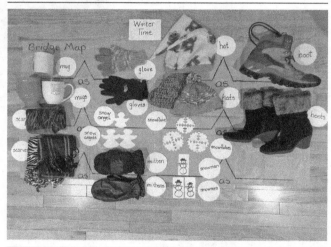

word usage such as singular and plural nouns related to winter (Figure 3.16).

To further challenge and deepen children's understanding of the book and wintertime concepts, read a second story, such as the children's classic *The Snowy Day* by Ezra Jack Keats (1962). Children can compare and contrast the two stories about wintertime using a large-group Double-Bubble Map to illustrate the similarities and differences (Figure 3.17).

Children can employ a Multi-Flow Map to visually sequence the cause–effect relationship of what happened to the snowball Peter placed in his pocket, when in the morning his pocket is wet

and the snowball is gone. Like the cooking experience with porridge, young children can investigate the states of matter as they observe what happens when ice cubes or crushed ice are placed at room temperature—physical science concepts discussed later in the chapter. To expand on children's understanding of winter in comparison to the other seasons, a Tree Map can be used to group and sort the different items and activities that take place during each season. Developmentally, it is important to emphasize that as learners become more fluent with all eight TMaps through the process of modeling,

Figure 3.17. Double-Bubble Map: Compare/Contrast *Snowballs* and *The Snowy Day*

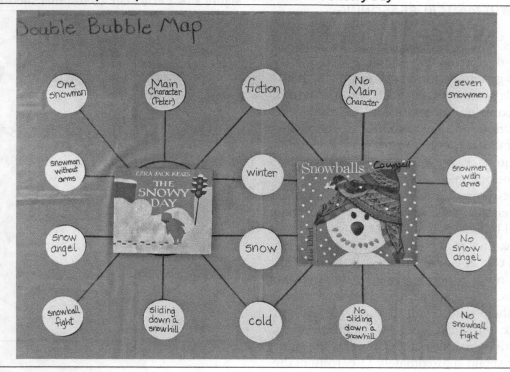

they develop visual consistency, flexible use, and the ability to integrate a range of different TMaps together according to the content they are learning and the text structures they have mastered in their own writing.

In addition to storybooks, young children often enjoy singing and dancing to familiar songs, as well as reciting nursery rhymes and fingerplays using flannel boards and puppets (McWilliams, 2017). Early childhood educators frequently write out the lyrics to songs children enjoy singing and acting out through role play, such as the "Wheels on the Bus," often sung at the beginning of the school year. Children can complete a variety of TMap activities related to this song. For example, children can use a Brace Map to document the part–whole relationships of buses (e.g., wheels, windows, door, seats); a Flow Map to sequence the series of events; and a Tree Map to classify different types of transportation (ground, air, water).

Even within many familiar songs, rhymes, and fingerplays, there can be multiple examples of how items function, with related causal mechanisms. In the case of the song "Wheels on the Bus," children can use a Bridge Map to specifically document the analogies of what happens (e.g., wheels go round and round; wipers go swish, swish, swish). Children can play with toy buses and other vehicles and observe how they move when they push them. These observations can be used to guide and inform deep and thoughtful discussions about the function of wheels (to help buses move on the ground) and causally relevant properties (circular objects roll). TMaps can be easily adapted to fingerplays and nursey rhymes, providing a context that allows for active physical engagement that may be even more appealing to some learners.

Storytime with young children can easily incorporate a variety of topics across content areas such as science and social studies. While it is true that the Brace, Tree, and Flow Maps encourage children to develop and use their logical-mathematical reasoning as they sequence, classify, and identify part–whole relationships, the different TMaps can be implemented to help children develop a variety of STEM skills and conceptual thinking beyond children's stories.

THINKING MAPS SUPPORT LOGICAL-MATHEMATICAL REASONING

Although it is widely accepted that mathematical thinking and development originates in the early years, math is generally not taught well using high-quality materials and activities with young children. One central contributing factor is the limited and weak preparation and professional development for teaching math experienced by early childhood educators who lack knowledge of mathematical content (Blömeke et al., 2011; NRC, 2010). In most preschool classrooms, little time is typically allocated to mathematics talk, rarely lasting longer than 1 minute, and limited to basic concepts such as numeral identification or names of shapes, with higher mathematical concepts rarely discussed (Rudd et al., 2008). While math concepts are embedded within puzzles, blocks, and board games, children may not fully utilize their mathematical thinking without adult guidance and facilitation (NRC, 2009).

In comparison to preschool settings, kindergarten classrooms spend approximately 11 percent of the school day learning mathematics. However, kindergartners also spend more time on low-level competencies such as geometric shapes and verbal counting using kindergarten curricula that fails to build mathematical competencies (Claessens et al., 2014). This is most unfortunate in light of the evidence that most children benefit from access to more advanced content (Claessens et al., 2014; Engel et al., 2013). Even in primary grades, where children often spend 90 minutes or more on mathematics, the quality of instruction and concepts are often not high.

TMaps can support and improve the quality of mathematical instruction with basic and more advanced math content in preschool, kindergarten, and primary grade classrooms, like the Tree Map used to classify the key items in *Goldilocks and the Three Bears*, according to seriations and double-seriations discussed earlier. Nationwide, teachers who have participated in professional learning workshops have uploaded vivid samples of maps completed with children to the Thinking Maps, Inc. website. Some of the shared maps are focused on the familiar basic concepts of counting and subitizing by having children brainstorm what they know about specific amounts using Circle or Flow Maps (Figures 3.18–3.19). The other major mathematical concept of

Figure 3.18. Circle Map: Conceptual Subitizing "6"

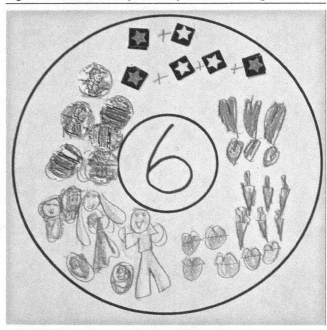

Figure 3.19. Flow Map: Conceptual Subitizing and Counting "6–10"

shapes (Figure 3.20) and three-dimensional solids (Figure 3.21) are grouped and sorted using Tree Maps. Children further apply their understanding of shape as they sort items shaped in an identical or similar way (such as an ice cream cone).

Advanced mathematical concepts explored and practiced using TMaps include children adding amounts sequentially with regrouping using a Flow Map (Figure 3.22).

Figure 3.20. Tree Map: Classifying Geometric Shapes

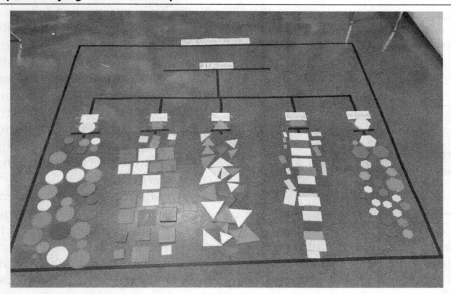

Figure 3.21. Tree Map: Classifying Three-Dimensional Solids by Shape

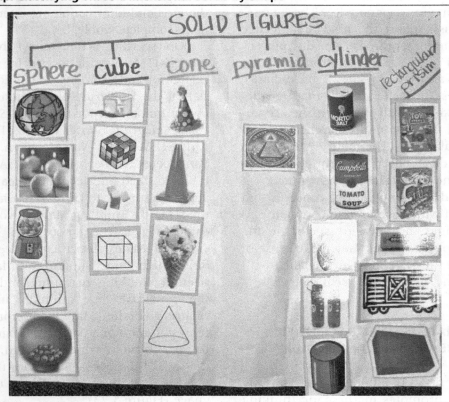

Figure 3.22. Flow Map: Sequencing Adding With Regrouping

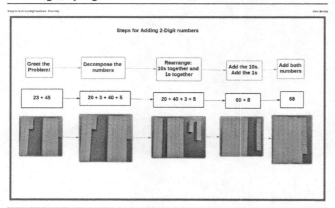

During TMap activities with young children, it is imperative that teachers exercise flexibility with allowing children to choose which TMap they want to use for a specific purpose, with some variation in the information included and how the information is conveyed using words, symbols, drawings, photos, and objects. Additionally, as learners decide which TMap(s) to use, it is equally important for teachers to constantly ask guiding questions, such as: How are you thinking about this (content)? Which TMaps are you going to use, and why? These metacognitive questions support the kind of reflective thinking and reasoning required across disciplines.

Characteristics of learning environments, as noted by Clements and Sarama (2012), that enhance children's attitudes and beliefs about mathematics are likewise compatible with the eight metacognitive processes and the Frame of Reference used in Thinking Maps (Table 3.2). The many TMap examples with real-world applications help children to vividly visualize and appreciate just how much they are immersed in mathematical concepts and processes, many of which are used to complete and support daily routines and activities (such as telling time and making purchases) as they make sense of the modern world they live in, which is filled with science, engineering, design, and technology.

THINKING MAPS PROMOTE SCIENTIFIC THINKING, REASONING, AND INQUIRY

The same characteristics of a high-quality learning environment that promotes mathematic thinking and learning will likewise support the attainment of the skill sets needed for economic success in the 21st century. The National Research Council's 2010 report, *Exploring the Intersection of Science Education and 21st Century Skills*, identified five skill sets critical to future job performance and economic success: (1) adaptability, (2) complex communications, (3) nonroutine problem solving, (4) self-management, and (5) systems thinking. TMaps are highly adaptable to accommodate different learners' age, development, ability, and language across content areas.

The eight TMaps and frame encourage complex communications using higher-order, open-ended questions while expanding children's vocabulary and usage. Problem solving is at the center of Thinking Maps regardless of which metacognitive process is used. Children's metacognition is not only foundational to scientific thinking (Kuhn, 2011) but also crucial to developing their self-management (self-regulation and inhibitory control) as they better understand and internalize "how" they learn. As children and teachers use the various TMaps to teach and learn about different content, their schema of understanding systematically helps them to make connections and see how the facts and information are interrelated to create a more complete whole.

One specific teaching model, the Inquiry Teaching Model (ITM), was developed by the Iowa Regents' Center for Early Developmental Education (IRCEDE) staff at the University of Northern Iowa and served as the framework for the guide *STEM Learning with Young Children* (Counsell et al., 2016) and subsequent early STEM guides (Van Meeteren, 2022a and 2022b; Van Meeteren & Peterson, 2022). As an actively child-centered, child-directed inquiry learning and teaching approach specific to early STEM in Pre-K–2 settings, the ITM, like Thinking Maps, advocates for a nonlinear learning–teaching process.

The ITM describes the practices (what educators do) to help guide, support, and facilitate children's scientific thinking, reasoning, and learning. Beyond the sequentially linear thinking used with the Flow Map, each of the TMaps is a nonlinear visual–spatial representation of a particular cognitive process and pattern through which children, as referenced in the title of the book, "draw out their learning" beyond oral and written and even mathematical language (Figure 3.23).

Table 3.2. Science and Mathematics Quick Content Correlations

QUICK CONTENT CORRELATIONS		
SCIENCE	**MAP**	**MATHEMATICS**
• Generating prior knowledge about a scientific concept • Searching for context information about a problem • Investigating scientific problems from multiple frames		• Defining a problem in context • Generating possible solutions to a problem • Putting word problems in context
• Describing properties of things • Identifying essential properties of an organism • Establishing criteria (value) for experimentation		• Identifying properties of numbers • Describing attributes of geometric figures • Establishing criteria for evaluation
• Comparing and contrasting properties of things • Comparing different systems • Comparing results from changes during experiments		• Comparing attributes of numbers • Comparing geometric figures • Evaluating alternative problem-solving approaches
• Creating categories (taxonomies), grouping items • Applying deductive and inductive reasoning • Organizing information during research		• Grouping types of numbers according to attributes • Classifying types of geometric figures • Sorting types of information in word problems
• Identifying whole-to-part relationships • Analyzing the anatomy of organisms • Creating new physical structures		• Analyzing spatial relationships • Identifying fractional references • Analyzing geometric figures
• Following directions in a scientific experiment • Logically organizing and prioritizing data • Analyzing the physiology of organisms		• Sequencing and ordering numbers • Following order of operations and steps • Reading and creating computer flow charts
• Analyzing cause(s) and effect(s) of events • Hypothesizing and predicting outcomes • Analyzing feedback in dynamic settings		• Following "if–then" propositions • Identifying causal relationships in word problems • Tracing causes and effects during problem solving
• Learning abstract concepts by analogy • Thinking relationally for creative problem solving • Inventing using analogical thinking		• Applying analogical reasoning • Solving problems using ratios and fractions • Using analogies for finding and solving problems

Figure 3.23. Inquiry Teaching Model (adapted from Counsell et al., 2016)

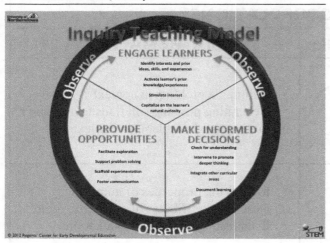

Providing young children with interesting, open-ended, thought-provoking materials that offer them something to figure out is developmentally worth their time and effort; this is central to the ITM and is also compatible with how we approach the use of TMaps with young children. As a metacognitive learning and teaching framework, Thinking Maps is also based heavily on inquiry that not only complements but can further enhance and enrich children's inquiry learning as an effective inquiry practice.

Like the Inquiry Teaching Model, observation plays a key role in the selection and implementation of TMaps to support and promote young children's scientific thinking and reasoning. Educators' observations not only provide vital assessment data concerning children's learning and development (as discussed in Chapter 5), observations are used continuously throughout the inquiry learning–teaching process.

During engagement in the ITM, much like TMaps with young children, interesting, open-ended, thought-provoking materials (especially those with causally relevant properties) are provided to intentionally invite children's exploration and encourage learning—an approach supported by current and ongoing research (Booth, 2009; Gopnik & Nazzi, 2003; Gopnik & Schulz, 2007). Educators also ask questions and provide additional materials according to their observations and children's responses to questions as they actively engage with TMaps.

These same observations provide critical information that reveal children's goals and agendas concerning what they want to do, make happen, and essentially learn about or understand. As a critical visual-spatial-language framework, TMaps create ongoing learning opportunities that actively foster children's problem solving as they help scaffold children's thinking and reasoning throughout the inquiry learning–teaching process. When combined with open-ended questions, such as productive questioning, TMaps can provide an authentic and compelling framework for communicating ideas while increasing children's vocabulary and usage. When the rectangular Frame of Reference is added around each TMap, an opening is offered for learner voice about how their own lives and prior knowledge influence the learning experience.

When combined with teachers' observations and productive questioning, TMaps provide additional information and insights that further support educators' informed decisions as they check for children's understanding; intervene to promote deeper thinking; integrate content curricula; and document their learning. Not only do TMaps provide critical insights into children's current thinking, reasoning, knowledge, and understanding in relation to science and other content areas, but more importantly, they reveal and promote children's deeper thinking according to the eight metacognitive processes specifically. For it is not simply how a learner uses each singular TMap but the degree to which they begin to orchestrate the transfer of multiple patterns of thinking together independently and collaboratively.

Children construct many ideas about how the world (both manmade and natural) works. As noted long ago by Piaget (1952), children are like "little scientists" who never tire as they explore and seek explanations. When confronted with novel objects (such as cove molding used as ramps), children will spontaneously ask questions with great persistence (Alvarez & Booth, 2014; Greif et al., 2006; Shavlik et al., 2020).

Children's interest and preference to learn by doing through direct, firsthand experiences are exemplified during scientific investigations and inquiry-based learning. High-quality investigations empower children to test their hypotheses and implicit theories about living and nonliving things, as well as physical causality (Samarapungavan et al., 2011). As children investigate, they can collect and interpret data patterns, with some understanding toward possible conclusions (Klahr & Chen, 2003).

As noted earlier, young children's knowledge of math is generally low, as is true of science (Gonzales et al., 2008; Greenfield et al., 2009; Kermani & Aldemir, 2015; Nayfield et al., 2011), especially when children reside in communities with limited resources. The frequency and duration of teaching science in kindergarten does not appear to predict science achievement at the end of 3rd grade (Sackes et al., 2011) or 8th grade (Sackes et al., 2013) in the United States, but the same is not true in other countries (Tao et al., 2012). Evidence suggests that the general low level of content and quality of instruction and curricula are contributing factors that must be addressed (Gerde et al., 2013; Henrichs et al., 2011). This includes greater emphasis on physics over simple biology and more conceptually rich activities (that TMaps can provide) over simple hands-on activities (Sackes et al., 2011).

In this book we recommend materials and activities designed to increase young children's active engagement with TMaps, as well as the eight metacognitive processes that directly connect to and help young children learn and understand STEM content. Nonetheless, it is imperative that we make it transparently clear that the learning–teaching experiences with TMaps should not be a substitution for children's active explorations and investigations. It is imperative that teachers carefully choose when to use TMaps to deepen, expand, enhance, and enrich discussions without leading, dictating, or directing children's thinking and understanding.

Even when educators teach science to young children, the tendency is to use general rather than domain-specific vocabulary (Henrichs et al., 2011) that TMaps can actively promote while enriching reading achievement. While Thinking Maps provide an important metacognitive framework for vocabulary development, TMap activities should not limit STEM teaching and learning to mere word recognition. Instead, Thinking Maps help children to communicate and explain the mental relationships they are constructing, and as such, teachers must choose carefully when to use them to guide and facilitate this process without explicitly direct-teaching those relationships to children. In brief, the cognitive processes of TMaps directly correspond to fundamental science processes:

- Context: Ecosystem
- Describing: Properties
- Comparing: Properties and other processes/supporting classifying
- Classifying: Taxonomy
- Whole–Part: Anatomy
- Sequencing: Cause–Effect: Physiology
- Analogies: Reasoning by analogy

Science Coming to "Life" With Thinking Maps

Simply stated, life sciences entail the study of living organisms and life processes. As noted earlier, animals are one of the most common topics among children's books. Some research even suggests that young children may prefer expository (informational) texts over narrative books (Kotaman & Tekin, 2017; Robertson & Reese, 2017). Other research indicates that children are drawn to picture books with familiar images that are colorful and representational rather than abstract (Danko-McGhee & Slutsky, 2011). Both educators and parents must keep in mind that we will always find both similar and unique preferences among individual children. Rather than overgeneralize our assumptions regarding what kinds of stories children will or will not be interested in reading, this evidence provides a poignant reminder to parents and teachers that it is critical to provide a balanced and diverse range of books for children to read and experience. At the same time, this research supports what many early childhood educators have believed and practiced for quite some time: that STEM content provides an ideal context for promoting young children's reading, writing, and talking in general, and as they relate to scientific literacy specifically.

While more and more children's books are exploring a wide assortment of STEM topics and concepts in general, no domain has been covered more than life sciences. Causally relevant properties pertaining to plant and/or animal life include nutritional needs/eating habits, aspects of inheritance and growth, habit, and social behavior. This causal information links cause–effect relationships in meaningful ways that young children can understand, relate to, and appreciate. Children's interest in conceptual knowledge (Gelman, 2003; Kelemen et al., 2003) and causal information draws on their attention/focus (inhibitory control), which in turn helps to facilitate preschoolers' acquisition of new words (Booth, 2009) and subsequent memory.

Just as it is critical to strategically determine when to bring children's literature into the learning–teaching process (e.g., to engage children's prior knowledge/experience, interest, and/or curiosity about a selected topic), it is equally imperative to mindfully determine when to best use Thinking Maps to deepen, enrich, and expand children's thinking. Children are immersed in a world surrounded by STEM concepts and relationships. Active exploration and investigation must be at the front and center of science teaching and learning with young children. Children's literature and TMaps are best used to support and promote children's explorations and investigations—not as a substitute in place of them.

The surrounding world is a child's classroom, and as children encounter animal and plant life, they are eager to learn where plants and animals come from, which plants are edible, and which animals like to eat different plants. Indoor and outdoor gardening experiences provide ample opportunities to explore how plants grow, what plants need to grow, how to care for plants, and how to harvest the edible parts of plants (Counsell et al., 2020). Children can also visit a local farm, greenhouse, florist shop, or botanical garden to learn about different types of plants.

Children and teachers can complete any combination of TMaps to think about, discuss, explain, and document the various mental relationships they have observed, experienced, and constructed based on the different gardening activities, investigations, field trips, and children's books. For example, after growing indoor or outdoor flowers, children take apart a flower and, using a Brace Map, name the parts of the plant, such as a tulip (Figure 3.24). Again, it is important to reiterate that scientific literacy entails more than simply naming items. After completing the Tulip Brace Map, children and teachers can discuss the position of each part of the plant, and children must be afforded the opportunity to explain how each part functions. For example, a tulip's roots are located at the bottom of the plant, anchoring it into the soil, and absorbing water and nutrients needed to live. Increasingly, research is indicating that educators and parents need to encourage

Figure 3.24. Brace Map: Parts of a Tulip in Spanish and English

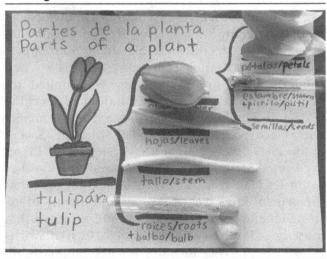

Figure 3.25. Brace Map: Parts of a Tree (Large Group)

young children to self-generate causal explanations in order to best promote causal learning and hypothesis revision (Booth et al., 2020; Legare & Lombrozo, 2014; Marcis & Sobel, 2017; Walker et al., 2017; Willard et al., 2019). In addition to Brace Maps about other plants (Figures 3.25 and 3.26), they can sequence plant harvesting, seed germination, and plant life cycles using Flow Maps (Figures 3.27 and 3.28). The Double-Bubble and Tree Maps challenge children to think critically and analytically about more complex features and attributes as they identify similarities and differences.

Figure 3.26. Brace Map: Parts of a Tree (Individual)

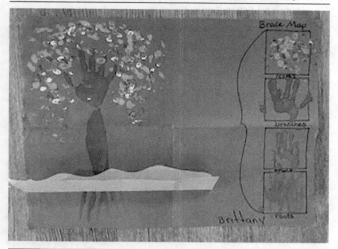

Figure 3.28. Flow Map: Sequencing the Apple Tree Life Cycle

Figure 3.27. Flow Map: Sequencing Seed Germination

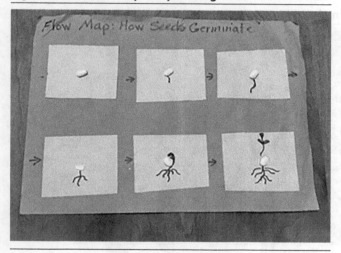

Figure 3.29. Tree Map: Classifying Living Organisms and Nonliving Items

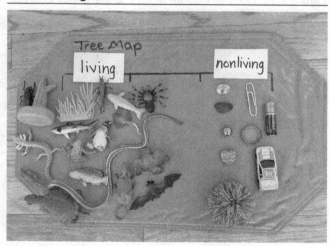

Children can engage in rich conversations as they classify plants and animals into groups based on causally relevant properties such as eating habits and social behaviors as well as other specified criteria (e.g., living or nonliving, vertebrates or invertebrates, born alive or hatched from eggs) using Tree Maps (Figures 3.29–3.31) or compare and contrast animal and plant life using Double-Bubble Maps (Figure 3.32). Children can be further challenged to use Multi-Flow Maps to examine cause–effect relationships, such as the contributing factors that cause plants to die (Figure 3.33). Early causal reasoning (as emulated here and in earlier examples

using TMaps) contributes toward the critical foundation upon which children develop scientific literacy (Shavlik et al., 2022).

Increased Environmental and Earth Awareness With Thinking Maps

Children's growing understanding of the fragility of life expands into an increasing awareness of our environment and the urgent need to protect it. Promoting environmental awareness (within physical science) encourages young children's sense of stewardship as they begin to understand and explain

Figure 3.30. Tree Map: Classifying Vertebrates and Invertebrates

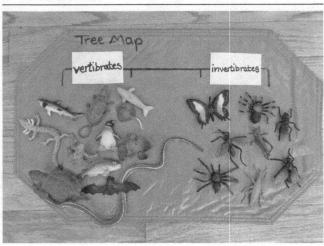

Figure 3.31. Tree Map: Classifying Animals Born Alive or Hatched From Eggs

Figure 3.32. Double-Bubble Map: Compare and Contrast Animal and Plant Life

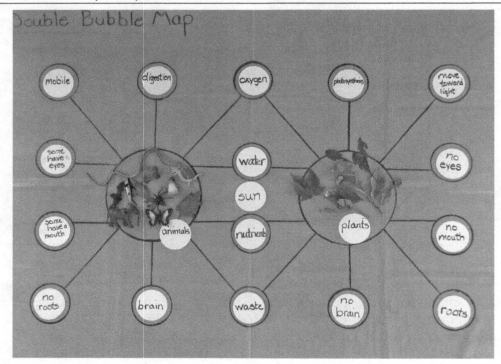

at a very early age how air pollution, water pollution, and land pollution negatively impact their world.

Children can use the Multi-Flow Map to communicate the cause–effect relationship that pollution has on the environment and Double-Bubble Maps to compare and contrast each type of pollution. Children can group and sort the different types of pollution or related concepts, such as sorting biodegradable and non-biodegradable items using a Tree Map (Figure 3.34) as they learn about, explore, and investigate recycling and composting. As children sort biodegradable and non-biodegradable items (see Counsell et al., 2017), teachers can ask the six types of productive questions (Elstgeest, 2001; Martens, 1999) to help facilitate their reasoning and scientific thinking (see Table 3.3). Children's pattern of question

Figure 3.33. Multi-Flow Map: Extreme Factors Causing Plants to Die

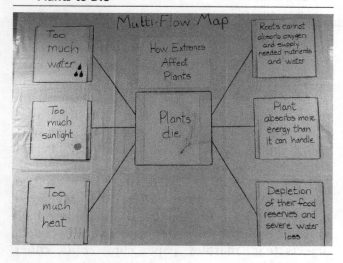

asking is significantly relevant to their scientific literacy development (Booth et al., 2020). It is likely that effective question asking is essential to knowledge acquisition across domains. Targeting causal information regarding concepts and mechanisms is arguably at the heart of scientific knowledge (Butler, 2020; Mills et al., 2019) and thereby, explanation and understanding in this manner is central to the scientific inquiry process itself (Jirout & Zimmerman, 2015; NRC, 2013; Schwarz et al., 2017).

Earth science is an area within physical science that entails studying the solid Earth, the water on and within it, and the air around it. In Earth science, concepts that young children can readily observe include clouds and soil. As children look up at the clouds, educators can discuss and help them describe what they see, eventually classifying the different types of clouds with Tree Maps (e.g., stratus, cirrus, cumulus). After children observe and explore different types of soil outside by digging, feeling, and smelling it, they can compare and contrast the types of soil they explore with Double-Bubble Maps (e.g., sand vs. clay).

Figure 3.34. Tree Map: Classifying Biodegradable and Non-Biodegradable Items

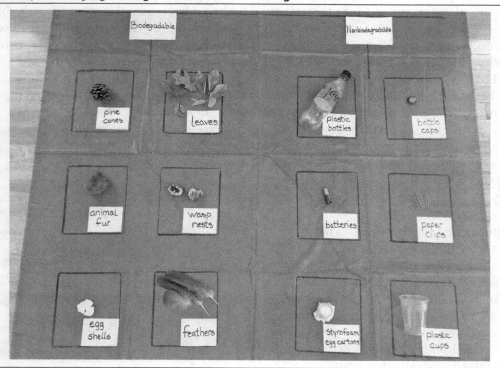

Table 3.3. Productive Questioning Guides and Facilitates Sorting Biodegradable and Non-Biodegradable Items

Types of Questions	Examples
Attention Focusing	What do you notice about the items that are biodegradable?
Measuring and Counting	How many of the items are non-biodegradable?
Comparison	Which items support a healthy environment? Which items create an unhealthy environment?
Action	What happens to biodegradable items left in the soil?
Problem Posing	How can we make the soil healthy for plants and animals?
Reasoning	Can you invent a rule to help keep the soil healthy for plants and animals?

For older children in primary grades who have developed as full conservers, they can begin to conceptualize the water cycle, observing what happens to rain puddles when the sun comes out and document the condensation-evaporation using either Flow or Multi-Flow Maps.

Getting "Physical" With Science Using Thinking Maps

In contrast to life science, physical science is a branch of natural science that studies the inorganic, nonliving systems with a focus on physics chemistry, Earth science, and astronomy. As a body of knowledge (content) and a way of knowing (process), science includes both concepts and inquiry. Like life science, children are also surrounded by physical science that affords many opportunities for exploration and investigation, with a few distinct and notable advantages. While life science investigations generally require adult guidance and supervision, young children can be successful in completing many kinds of open-ended physical science activities independently with minimal adult supervision. DeVries and Sales (2011) recommend using the following four criteria to develop high-quality physical science experiences that children complete independently:

- Producible: Children "produce" what happens with their own actions.
- Immediate: Children experience what happens "immediately" in response to their actions.
- Observable: Children "observe" (see, hear, feel, smell, or taste) what happens in response to their actions.
- Variable: Children "vary" their actions and/or materials to observe what happens.

Ramps and Pathways is an approach to early physical science that is guided and informed by constructivist theory. As young children build ramp structures and pathways with lengths of cove molding, they explore and investigate what will happen as they release marbles on their structures (Counsell, 2011, 2017; Counsell et al., 2013; Counsell et al., 2016; Counsell & Geiken, 2019; DeVries & Sales, 2011; Van Meeteren, 2022b; Zan & Geiken, 2010). After children have multiple opportunities to release a variety of solid objects (e.g., marbles, paper clips, coins, cubes, cotton balls, buttons) on inclined planes using cove molding, extensively exploring and investigating with force and motion, they can then engage in stimulating conversations about what they observe and experience. Bubble Maps can help children to focus on and describe the specific attributes of each object (Figure 3.35). While

Figure 3.35. Bubble Map: Describing the Attributes of a Marble

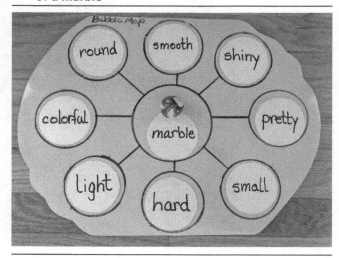

perceptual qualities may be relatively easy for young children to identify, it is the causally relevant properties centered on the object's function that appear to be the most interesting, attention-focusing, motivating, and thus most memorable for young children (Booth, 2009; Booth et al., 2020; Shavlik et al., 2020).

As children observe how different objects move, their interest, attention, and motivation increase as they witness how the causally relevant properties (such as round and circular) are used in an object's design in order to satisfy the object's function (e.g., marbles roll). Children's explorations and investigations with multiple items provide important opportunities to construct mental relationships concerning how an object's shape (a causally relevant property) dictates how it will move (cause–effect relationship).

Double-Bubble Maps can help facilitate children's attention (inhibitory control) to the causally relevant property of motion as they think about, reflect on, compare, contrast, and explain their observations of two different objects (Figure 3.36). To further challenge children's understanding of the causality relationship of shape and motion, children can think about, discuss, and classify multiple objects according to their shape and motion (e.g., roll, slide, tumble,

spin) using a Tree Map (Figure 3.37). Additional analysis can be conducted as children take the same causal properties and relationships utilized in the Tree Map and transfer and apply the cause–effect relationships to the Bridge Map to further think about, discuss, document, and explain the object–motion analogies, such as "marbles roll" and "cubes slide" (Figure 3.38).

Figure 3.36. Double-Bubble Map: Compare and Contrast Motion Objects

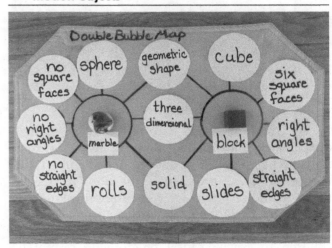

Figures 3.37 and 3.38. Tree Maps: Classifying Objects by Motion

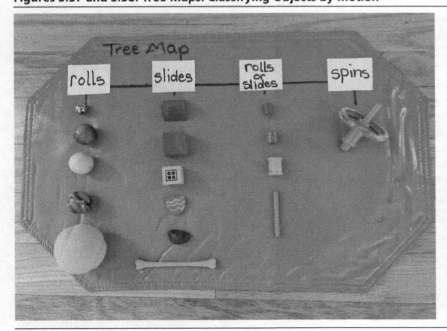

Photo courtesy of SWTCC—Union Campus Child Care Center

Figure 3.39. Bridge Map: Analyzing Motion–Object Analogies

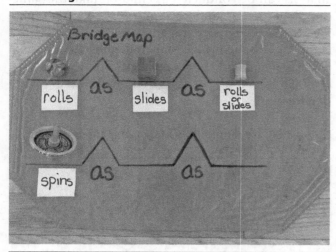

As children engage with different maps, such as a Bridge Map to help them analyze the relationship between shape and motion (Figure 3.39), teachers can ask productive questions as needed to guide and facilitate their scientific thinking and reasoning (see Table 3.4).

The need for parents and educators to invite children to *explain* causal phenomena cannot be overstated. While the frequency with which parents reference causal information (causal talk) in their speech may help to predict the strength of children's causal stance, it is the frequency with which children are invited to explain causal phenomena that may best support scientific literacy (Bauer & Booth, 2019; Booth et al., 2020) in early childhood and beyond. The power of self-generated explanation advances STEM learning significantly, especially within the context of causal phenomenon (Bonawitz et al.,

2011; Legare et al., 2016). When children generate explanations, they use the evidence they have at hand as they connect their understanding with how the world works (Busch et al., 2018). The inconsistencies and questions that emerge compel children toward further exploration until they figure out what is happening, empowering them to find solutions to the problems encountered, thus proving to be a particularly promising approach (Booth et al., 2020).

ENGINEERING DESIGN AND TECHNOLOGY WITH THINKING MAPS

Science and engineering practices include activities that promote scientific knowledge acquisition such as asking questions, planning and carrying out investigations, and analyzing and interpreting data. As children design and construct increasingly complex ramp structures, for example, they use engineering design as they:

1. Ask what they want the marble to do
2. Imagine how they will need to position the ramps and blocks (or other supports)
3. Plan which materials to use and the sequence for construction
4. Create the structure
5. Test the structure by releasing the marble and observing what happens
6. Improve the structure by making needed adjustments to achieve the desired outcome, such as making the marble turn a corner (Counsell et al., 2016; DeVries & Zan, 2012; Van Meeteren, 2022b)

Table 3.4. Productive Questioning Guides and Facilitates the Analysis of Motion Items

Types of Questions	Examples
Attention Focusing	What do you notice about the items that roll?
Measuring and Counting	Which items move faster, objects that roll or slide?
Comparison	Which items roll? Which items slide?
Action	How do cylinders move when placed vertically on the inclined plane?
Problem Posing	How can we make spheres roll faster?
Reasoning	Why do you think cubes slide?

The more young children investigate with Ramps and Pathways, the more confident they become in their engineering design and their willingness to integrate different technologies into their design plans.

Technology generally refers to "any modification of the natural world made to fulfill human needs or desires" (Gamire & Pearson, 2006, p. 1). In addition to using wooden cove molding for the ramps, other technologies include tubing, Hot Wheels tracks, fulcrums, cardboard boxes, different spheres, Matchbox cars, and containers for catching objects.

A child's modern world is filled with ever-increasing technologies that were developed using engineering design. As young engineers, children can use Flow Maps to document the design process as they construct and create new and familiar technologies (such as a car). Their selection of materials (including the shape of different parts) is guided and informed by children's physical knowledge of causal relevant properties and their cause–effect relationships in order to achieve the design purpose or function (Figure 3.40).

Throughout the day, children use an assortment of technologies to expediently perform a variety of daily tasks, routines, and activities, such as eating utensils during mealtime and grooming and hygiene items in the morning or bedtime. The various Thinking Maps can be easily employed to enrich and deepen children's existing funds of knowledge based on their prior experiences to fully understand and appreciate how and why they were invented by using engineering design to improve our daily lives, both historically and across regions and cultures.

Figure 3.40. Flow Map: Sequencing a Toy Car Design Process

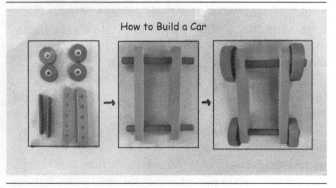

SOCIAL STUDIES INSTRUCTION AND THINKING MAPS

Key topics or units of study in social studies with young children include history, citizenship, economics, and geography. Young children often accompany their parents to voting polls during local, state, and national elections. They also see candidates' names and images on signs, flags, and billboards and in TV ads. They hear elected executive and legislative officials speaking to reporters and audiences. Many Pre-K–2 learners can tell you the name of the current U.S. president, and they often know which candidates their parents prefer.

Together in small- and large-group arrangements, children can complete Circle and Bubble Maps to brainstorm and describe what they know about specific public offices such as the president, noting the roles and duties of the office (nation's leader) as well as specific characteristics (Figures 3.41–3.42).

When children are communicating their prior knowledge and understanding of concepts and ideas, it is important to ensure that each child has full access to voice and agency as they actively share during group discussions, as further elaborated in the next chapter. However, in the case of the TMap below, children were combining facts (e.g., the Oval Office) with adjectives (Figure 3.43). To avoid confusing learners about the metacognitive process they are using as they think, talk, and write about a topic, in this instance, it would be more accurate and helpful to provide another large sheet of paper. When children state facts, the teacher could ask, "Does that describe a characteristic of the President, or is it a fact about the President's roles and responsibilities?" Once learners determine whether it belongs on a Bubble Map, the teacher can ask, "What TMap can we use to document that information?" Children's faces will light up as they realize, "A Circle Map!" A child can volunteer to draw a large outer circle and inside circle and write any facts they know on that TMap. In this way, all children's voices are honored and their agency has been granted to act on their ideas. The discussion that ensues becomes even more dynamic and stimulating as the cooperative group works on two TMaps simultaneously, actively using their metacognitive skills and cognitive flexibility as they shift back and

Figures 3.41 and 3.42. Bubble Maps: Describing the Office of the President (Group Work)

Photos courtesy of Bartlett Elementary School Kindergarten Class.

Figures 3.43. Bubble Map: Describing the Office of the President Completed

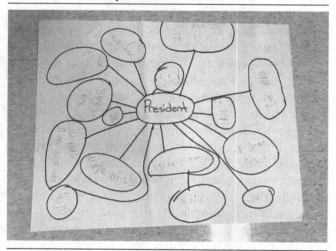

forth from one cognitive process (describing) to another (brainstorming).

After reading literature and taking field trips to local courthouses and state capitol buildings, children can revisit their completed TMaps to check for accuracy and add missing facts and details. As they learn about the three branches of government, they can use a Tree Map to classify the roles and responsibilities of each branch or complete a Flow Map to sequence the steps for how a bill becomes federal law.

Children's investigations into the engineering design of familiar technologies can readily evolve into historical perspectives concerning the origins of human-made technology. Familiar technology used by children in their daily lives, such as eating utensils, can readily lead to inquisitive explorations into the earliest origins, such as the oldest bowl artifact found, the material used, and the bowl's design purpose (e.g., to prepare food in or to eat from). Geographically, a variety of bowls and utensils have been designed for different purposes depending on the indigenous plants and animals that are consumed. Clearly, the Thinking Map applications used to enhance and enrich children's critical and analytical reasoning and discourse across literacy, math, and science content likewise intersects and overlaps with social studies content in ways that are equally purposeful, meaningful, and relevant.

History With Thinking Maps

Children's notion of history begins with their individual life stories within their families. This includes a timeline from when they were born in relation to older and younger siblings, and family pets with major life events, cultural celebrations, and traditions. Children can complete individual TMaps and then compare and contrast the similarities and differences with their classmates. Thinking Maps can help children mindfully identify and appreciate their own multiple identities (e.g., a daughter, sister, best friend, neighbor, kindergartner, Muslim, dual language learner, soccer player, scout, violinist). Collectively, the individual life stories come together to form a rich, complex, and diverse learning community (as further discussed in Chapter 4).

As children learn about their classmates, their notion of history expands beyond their family and neighborhood communities. This increased scope can then be applied to broader applications of history of the town, city, state, region, and nation where children reside, examining historical figures and events using the different TMaps.

Geography With Thinking Maps

In many ways, geography provides an ideal context for teachers to develop units of study. Before children can understand the people, lifestyles, and activities in other parts of the world, they must first develop a strong sense of self (identity), lived experiences, and the world in which they live. Their prior knowledge and experiences with their own local history, citizenship, and economics serves as the foundation upon which they construct and extend new understanding about the people, places, and things in other parts of the world in relation to their own.

Teachers can readily integrate literacy, math, and science skills and concepts into geography units of study as children examine and learn about different countries and continents, climate, topography, indigenous plants and animals, and natural resources available, using TMaps to guide and facilitate rich discussions. Children can read books about the types of plants that are harvested in particular regions (literacy); study the size of populations, amount of food harvested, and general consumption per individual (math); and discuss factors related to the planting seasons, soil quality, climate, weather, and the resulting health and nutrition of the human populations dependent on the food source (science).

Before reading about a dominant food staple grown in a geographic region, children can brainstorm what they know (or think they know) about that crop using a Circle Map. After reading about that type of crop (such as wild rice), children can sample the food, steamed or boiled, and then complete a Bubble Map to describe it using their five senses (i.e., color, flavor, aroma, texture). Children can complete a Double-Bubble Map comparing and contrasting it to a similar food or strain (such as white rice) that they eat and how it may be prepared differently (cooked and seasoned). Flow Maps can sequence

the planting and harvesting season, the plant's life cycle, or a cooking recipe, and a Multi-Flow Map can explore the cause–effect relationship of hazardous weather systems or insect infestations. Tree Maps can be used to group and sort harvested crops according to their countries or continents of origin.

RELATED EARLY CHILDHOOD APPROACHES AND CURRICULA

Generally speaking, a curricular approach is less detailed than a model. Approaches (like the Project Approach) describe the main elements or direction of a program (Roopnarine & Johnson, 2008). As illustrated above, TMaps can easily support and complement content learning and instruction across primary grade curricula. TMaps are equally valuable with young children in preschool settings as well, using widely accepted and implemented early childhood curricula that similarly follow a project-focused teaching–learning approach.

The Reggio Emilia Approach Makes Learning Visible

Rather than prescribe a model for others to imitate, Reggio Emilia educators (like the Project Approach) embrace a set of principles applied across contexts with diverse children, families, and educators (Griebling, 2011; Helm & Katz, 2011; Lewin-Benham, 2011). As such, it promotes a method for engaging young children with curriculum content. The Reggio Approach is based on an emergent curriculum that is largely guided and informed by children's interests, resulting in child-centered projects on selected topics.

Many Reggio Emilia educators have adopted the Project Approach as a useful framework to help facilitate children's project-based learning. Like the Project Approach, Reggio Emilia educators strive to help children make learning visible by spending extensive amounts of time gathering data, charting their progress, and documenting children's work using photos and videos (Jalongo & Isenberg, 2012). Maps help to make children's thinking visible and can thus be implemented during any phase of children's projects to stimulate and support their thinking. As a valuable resource for documentation, children's maps simultaneously serve as important communication tools that help them to share and discuss their ideas and gained information with peers and adults.

Traditionally, early childhood has prioritized the process of learning and instruction over content outcomes or products of what children learn. However, past decades of education reform dictated in large part by federally legislated mandates such as NCLB and Race to the Top have resulted in an explosion in early childhood curriculum development (Bredekamp, 2011).

Bank Street Approach

In contrast to learning approaches, a curriculum model refers specifically to a research-based framework for how to teach and the anticipated learning outcomes that should result. Also referred to as the Developmental Interaction Approach, Bank Street was heavily influenced by the Progressive Movement and emulated the philosophy of John Dewey during the first half of the 20th century, a time when children were expected to sit obediently at their desks, directed by the teacher as to when to listen, recite, or reply in unison.

Bank Street embraces the belief that children learn best from direct experiences with the outside world, which in turn produces rational, thoughtful citizens. Bank Street educators' efforts to capitalize on children's curiosity and motivation to learn about the world can be further supported and advanced using TMaps. Similar to the Reggio Emilia and Project Approach, Bank Street also encourages children to actively engage and interact with experiences in the world, such as understanding local, national, and global events. Child-centered learning often takes a project-based or problem-based approach to learning that is similar to the Reggio Emilia and the Project Approach.

Problem-based learning, like the Project Approach, empowers learners to identify real-world problems and questions that are worthy of exploration, leading to possible solutions. Regardless of the version of project work used, project work "incorporates facts and skills in the service of doing something that is as real and practical as it is intellectual and scholarly" (Kohn, 1999, p. 148). Once again, TMaps can be used to help identify problems worthy of investigation; organize facts and information into meaningful frameworks; and summarize what is learned, in order to propose possible solutions.

High/Scope Curriculum

Developed during the Perry Preschool Project in the early 1960s by David Weikart and colleagues, research studies have demonstrated High/Scope's lasting positive effects and children's long-term success in school and life (Schweinhart et al., 2005). Guided by the constructivist view about how children learn, High/Scope engages young children in active, engaged hands-on learning experiences with people, objects, activities, and ideas (Epstein, 2007).

Instead of a 3-Phase Project Approach framework designed to investigate and explore new topics, High/Scope organizes all learning according to a plan-do-review process. During children's 60–90 minutes of choice time, they plan what they will do, carry out those plans, and then review their plans, reflecting on what was learned and what they may want to do differently later. With a greater planning focus, children can also use maps to support each step of the process.

Creative Curriculum

Creative Curriculum, like High/Scope, is a child-centered curriculum model that focuses on the process of how children learn and develop according to constructivist theory. While Creative Curriculum also emphasizes children's play with child-initiated activities facilitated by educators, similar to the previously described approaches and models, Creative Curriculum places greater emphasis on the learning environment as the organizing framework. Over time, Creative Curriculum has evolved, drawing on various learning theorists—Maslow, Erikson, Piaget, and Vygotsky—to help inform how educators observe, reflect, and respond to children in ways that facilitate their learning and development (Copley, 2007; Dodge et al., 2004; Heroman & Jones, 2004).

Educators implementing this curriculum can help children to incorporate TMaps into the different center activities. For example, in the block center, children and educators can take photos or draw pictures of structures they create. They can then complete various maps to document and demonstrate what they can tell others about their structure. For example, children can dictate to educators different adjectives that describe their structure using a Bubble Map or sequence the blocks they used to build their structure using a Flow Map.

As child-centered curriculum models, both Creative Curriculum and High/Scope focus on the process of how children learn and develop from a constructivist perspective. One notable distinction is that High/Scope utilizes a plan-do-review process in contrast to the Creative Curriculum's heavier emphasis on the learning environment. High/Scope and Creative Curriculum are the two most common curricula used by Head Start (www.nhsa.org).

Tools of the Mind

More recently, the Tools of the Mind curriculum has been created and grounded in Vygotsky's sociocultural theory of learning for children Pre-K through 2nd grade (Bodrova & Leong, 2007). Based on the educator's role to guide and support children's learning and development within a child-centered environment, Tools of the Mind developed specific strategies designed to promote children's early literacy, self-regulation, and cognitive skill development. Tools of the Mind recognizes that children will likely struggle with learning academic skills if they lack critical "global" cognitive skills, such as self-regulation. Hence, educators strive to emphasize self-regulation in all classroom activities.

Similar to High/Scope, Tools of the Mind also engage children in play planning, but in this instance children describe their plans in writings or drawings specifically. Within this process, TMaps can help children to formulate and organize their plans. Making their cognitive thought patterns visible, children can combine drawings or photos with written language as they plan before, during, and after their play experience in much the same fashion as the plan-do-review process with High/Scope.

CONCLUSION

This chapter has demonstrated with detailed examples how teachers can effectively implement Thinking Maps across the content areas of literacy, math, science, and social studies in ways that enrich, enhance, and deepen children's learning and maximize the developmental outcomes needed for success in the 21st century. When used in ways that are meaningful, purposeful, and relevant to young children's interests, deep funds of knowledge, and prior experiences, the eight metacognitive processes promoted and visually represented by TMaps support teachers' efforts to help children learn deeper knowledge and understanding of core academic content that encourages children to apply skills and concepts across the academic domains.

Thinking Maps promote children's understanding and analytical reasoning as they actively engage the metacognitive strategies. TMaps' visual-language framework help children to critically and mindfully tackle novel problems and situations, particularly those encountered during scientific investigations and engineering design, while using a variety of technologies to help find solutions to the problems they encounter. As detailed above, across the disciplines, the eight universal cognitive processes unite into dynamic, consistent, and flexible patterns using the TMaps and Frame of Reference that easily transfer from story time in the morning to mathematics and science after a morning break, to history and social studies in the afternoon as a seamless language for learning. The five key attributes of TMaps combine to focus on the developmental aspects of learning for *all* students, leading to enhanced executive functioning and metacognition.

As discussed in Chapter 2 and further exemplified across the content areas, the learning and developmental benefits of Thinking Maps are maximized within democratic learning communities. TMaps help teachers to plan and prepare active engagement with rich, inclusive language discussions to ensure full participation from learners, who are encouraged to exercise their voice and agency throughout the teaching–learning process. In Chapter 4, more information about inclusive practices and recommendations for how to best differentiate instruction using a variety of accommodations and modifications for a full range of different learners during TMap activities will be extensively discussed and elaborated.

Thinking Maps Promote Democratic Learning Communities With Full Community Membership

After our third year in the Indianapolis project, the board of education summoned the assistant superintendent to explain why it should continue to fund the literacy initiative. We decided that the most convincing way to respond would be for teachers from kindergarten through high school to share with the board the effects of the strategies and practices they had been implementing in their classrooms. Every one of the teachers talked about the impact the Thinking Maps had on the achievement of their students: a kindergarten teacher presented samples of her students' studies in science through each of the eight Thinking Maps; middle school literacy teachers shared examples of student expository and narrative writings; a chemistry teacher demonstrated how he applied the maps in chemistry . . . and the real epiphany was experienced by the high school teacher, who exclaimed, "Wait! The kindergarten teachers are using the same apps we are. If every teacher is working on this kind of thinking with his or her students, think how strong they'll be by the time they get to high school" (Jackson, 2011, p. 60).

To help educators successfully implement Thinking Maps with a full range of learners, this chapter further demonstrates that the maps (1) qualify as an effective Universally Designed Learning curriculum; (2) help scaffold learning according to the zone of proximal development; and (3) support differentiated instruction with individualized accommodations and modifications. When educators focus on what is educationally relevant, rather than categorically ranking and sorting children based on deficit assumptions, teaching is more sensitive and respectful to the individual learner, and this in turn increases children's access to learning activities through more varied instruction (and intervention).

The following discussion is intended as a starting point and a place of departure. The goal is to use this information as a guiding framework, not as the end-all or be-all that could potentially limit, hinder, or impede children's access but instead to help educators recognize their potentially unchecked biased assumptions and move beyond them in order to maximize all learner outcomes within democratic learning communities.

THINKING MAPS PROMOTE RESPONSIVE, DEMOCRATIC LEARNING

Thinking Maps encourage inclusive learning experiences within positive, supportive, interactive, and engaging environmental settings. While all children exhibit responsiveness to environmental influences, a subset of children in particular demonstrate an associated susceptibility to the character of their social environments, but are very responsive to early interventions (Belsky & van Ijzendoorn, 2015). Educators must ensure that all children have full access to developmentally responsive and supportive environments using high-quality teaching and learning experiences like TMaps.

According to Wilson (n.d.), any formal education experience has three common key aspects: (1) materials and activities for children's engagement; (2) time allotted for engagement; and (3) a learning climate that either encourages or discourages active social interactions (child–adult interactions as well as peer interactions). The eight cognitive process TMaps and Frame of Reference, as described throughout this book, can be implemented in any grouping arrangement using a variety of materials. Whether children work in large, small, or paired groupings, they need to be using a variety of social-emotional skills in order to fully participate in the learning activity.

Children are generally eager to share their ideas, thoughts, and experiences within social learning arrangements promoted by TMaps. Most often, "sharing" consists of verbal communication, and many children—shy, insecure, not readily verbal, or speaking in a second language—do not feel comfortable verbalizing their thinking. TMaps offer a safe visual space for drawing children's learning out for others and then speaking from their graphic display. Many, if not a majority of our learners, especially in our visually saturated online world, are dominantly visual learners. A maximum learning experience means all children have equal opportunity to contribute to the class discussion and to ask and answer questions on the chosen topic.

Thinking Maps Are Intrinsically Motivating

As young children's thinking develops, they frequently connect their cognition to motivational features of their early learning. With age, children become more aware of how their performance compares to others and become increasingly sensitive to feedback from parents and teachers regarding their academic achievement. In turn, children translate that same feedback into their notion of self-confidence, intrinsic motivation, persistence, and other characteristics related to learning skills.

When *all* children are granted opportunities to make choices and decisions as well as to direct their inquiries according to their own interests and curiosities, as emulated in the ITM, *all* children are more likely to exert their fullest attention and mental energy toward finding answers to the questions that help them achieve goals and outcomes that matter most to them. The more children are empowered with an active voice to pursue their own queries and agency to act on their intellectual pursuits by choosing and completing relevant TMaps, the more they increase their self-confidence as capable learners.

Research reveals that children's self-confidence is an important predictor of academic success; it is therefore critical that teachers provide performance feedback in ways that empower children (Hamre, 2014). Materials and approaches that actively encourage children's voice and agency, like TMaps, communicate to learners that their thoughts, ideas, beliefs, and perspectives matter. *How* they think, and the explicit *discussion* of their processes becomes as important as *what* they *think* or can remember. As activities like TMaps elevate students' voices to the center of all learning, all children (1) are seen and heard as they articulate their ideas and thinking, (2) gain greater insight and understanding about how they learn best (metacognition), and (3) are empowered to demonstrate what they have learned in ways that interest them and tap into their strengths (www .hollyclark.org/2017/11/07/disrupting-the-students -role-in-the-classroom) (Figure 4.1).

Children's belief that their views and opinions matter further reinforces their self-worth, self-esteem, and self-identity as capable thinkers and learners. The common expression "I see what you mean" is realized in full when all learners can display the full patterns of their thinking beyond their verbal capacities to recall and articulate what they mean, and how they mean it.

As young children exert their voice using TMaps, they gain greater agency, placing them in the driver's seat as they make choices, and take purposeful initiative to independently complete the maps, which are increasingly extended to all learning. Together, children's voice and agency during TMaps promote

Figure 4.1. Student Voice—Key Aspects in Relation to TMaps

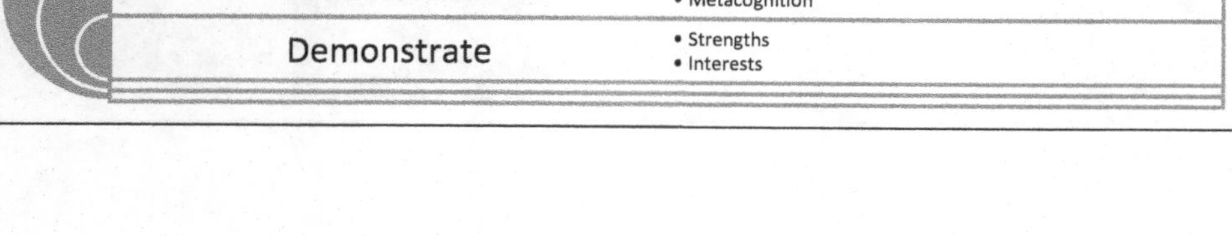

Articulate	• Ideas • Thinking
Understand	• Content • Metacognition
Demonstrate	• Strengths • Interests

learners' high agency within democratic learning communities in stark contrast to teacher-driven, teacher-centered teaching and learning that results in low agency for learners (Figure 4.2).

Consider how one 1st-grade teacher guided children to explore their notions of "self" in a unit study, "All About Me," according to their individual likes, interests, favorites, and daily home routines. Children used Circle Maps to brainstorm how they

see themselves in relation to their interests, hobbies, and favorites, suggesting the people, places, activities, and things that matter most to them. In addition to the required Circle Map (see the image on the book cover), the same student used a Brace Map to name the parts of her favorite outfit (Figure 4.3); a Flow Map to sequence the multiple tasks she completes to get ready for school (Figure 4.4); and a Multi-Flow Map to describe the cause–effect relationship of growing a pumpkin to enjoy in three distinct ways during one of her favorite holidays, Halloween (Figure 4.5).

Giving students the visual patterns to integrate the content and process of their learning into

Figure 4.2. Learner Agency: Low Agency vs. High Agency

Image courtesy of Christine McCormick-Liddle.

Figure 4.3. Brace Map: Parts of My Favorite Outfit

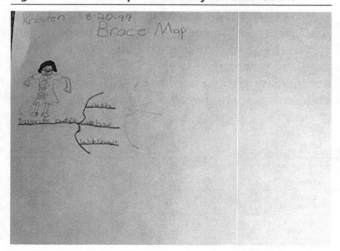

Figure 4.4. Flow Map: Sequencing Tasks to Get Ready for School

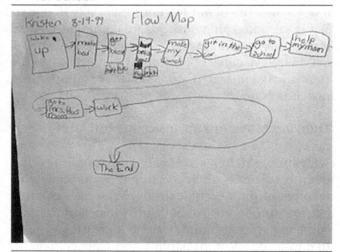

Figure 4.5. Multi-Flow Map: Cause-Effect With Pumpkins Used to Enjoy Halloween

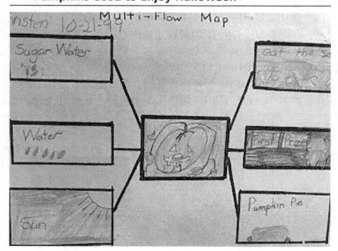

multiple displays of what may be called "visual sche-mas" help to draw out their deepest thinking about themselves and to literally see others' perspectives along the way.

Democratic membership, as defined by Kohn (1999, 2006), empowers children to (1) have a voice in what happens, (2) help shape the course of study, (3) help decide when, where, why, how, and with whom learning takes place, and (4) determine how progress will be assessed. When teachers listen at-tentively to children, they acknowledge children's prior knowledge, interests, agendas, and ideas. TMap activities promote democratic learning communities by mutually respecting and valuing all shared ideas, perspectives, and experiences (Counsell, 2011).

Children Least Likely to Experience Democratic Learning

Studies examining the relationship between socio-economic status (SES) and racial school demograph-ics further suggest a direct correlation with specific types of social climate, theoretical approaches, and teaching practices (classroom cultures) (Boykin et al., 2000; Stipek & Valentino, 2015). Teachers who work in low-income and high-poverty schools pre-dominantly use a Direct Instruction curricular and behaviorist approach to teaching and learning that emphasizes a classroom culture of discipline (Stipek & Valentino, 2015).

One study examining the nature of instruction used by 314 kindergarten and 1st-grade teach-ers (92% female; 73% White) across three states largely serving children of color from low-income families revealed that didactic, direct instruction with isolated basic skills emphasis and negative social climates dominated the teaching–learning experience (Stipek, 2004; Stipek & Valentino, 2015). Consequently, if these same children start school with fewer school readiness skills, they are at a greater risk for later struggles with academ-ic achievement (Reardon, 2011; Reardon et al., & Weathers, 2015).

Thinking Maps Encourage Cooperation and Collaboration

The introduction of cooperative learning and con-flict resolution continue to change and improve

the social learning dynamics of classroom com-munities. Hyerle (2009) commends educators who implement instructional strategies and materials that actively promote interactivity. Within socially dynamic classrooms, constructivist educators guide and facilitate children's construction of mental rela-tionships by (1) engaging children's interest, (2) in-spiring active exploration and investigation, and (3) fostering cooperation between adults and children and among peers (DeVries & Zan, 2012). Thinking Maps provide learners with a visual framework that helps them to make their mental relationships and patterns of thinking "visible."

As a model and approach, Thinking Maps sat-isfy the three key criteria for constructivist teaching practice. TMaps actively engage children's interest on any chosen topic; inspire children to complete multiple maps as they explore, investigate, and learn more about the topic; and foster cooperation be-tween adults and children and among peers. Hence, TMaps promote teachers and learners to "really think together" (Williams, 2011, p. 31) as they co-construct knowledge and mental relationships.

As a cooperative learning–teaching framework, TMaps help learners "transcend the sense of self" in order to enlarge the concept of "me" to a sense of "us" (Hyerle, 2009, p. xiii). Encouraging learners to become less attached to egocentric orientations per-mits them to exercise more advanced reasoning pro-cesses. As children (and adults) learn to transcend the self to become part of the whole, as asserted by Hyerle, they do not lose their individuality or no-tion of self but instead relinquish their egocentricity.

This is particularly heightened by the common use of the rectangular Frame of Reference drawn around each TMap as a reflective mirror for asking such questions as, What has influenced my think-ing? How are my emotions drawing out these ideas or possibly limiting my view? Which experiences are most impacting how I am thinking and feeling? How are others (peers in collaborative groups) af-fecting my thinking and feelings?

Working collaboratively with children as they mutually define how they want to operate, act, think, and learn as a community helps teachers to transform into "fellow travelers" as they co-construct meanings and relationships in a shared journey of learning, growth, and empowerment (Counsell & Boody, 2013). As children in the primary grades show more independence from their parents and family, they simultaneously place an increasing importance on friendship and being liked and accepted by peers. As children spend larger increments of time in learning environments, they begin to develop a greater sense and understanding of their place in that world (CDC, 2014).

The emotional support and security provided by positive relationships in the early years contributes in multifaceted ways to young children's learning and development. Children with secure adult attachments develop greater understanding of others, show more advanced moral development, and exhibit a more positive self-concept (Thompson, 2013). During the primary grades, children (especially those with secure attachments) make notable gains in (1) understanding their feelings, (2) learning how to more effectively express their thoughts and feelings, (3) wanting to play cooperatively, (4) striving to work in teams, and (5) attempting to resolve conflicts without adult intervention (CDC, 2014).

Since learning is inherently a social process, young children who develop secure relationships are more likely to fully invest themselves in learning. Children who have warm, quality relationships with secure attachments to educators experience increased confidence during learning and demonstrate greater regulatory competence with better learning overall (NICHD Early Child Care Research Network, 2005; Pianta & Stuhlman, 2004).

Thinking Maps Support Class Meetings. Children as young as preschool age can actively participate in class meetings. Community meetings are group times held at the beginning and end of the school day, as needed, to discuss issues or concerns related to class activities, community member interactions, or community rules, policies, or procedures. Generally speaking, class meetings provide children the opportunity to "exchange ideas in a respectful, caring atmosphere" (Styles, 2001, p. 7).

Class meetings, with teacher guidance, empower children to help identify issues, reflect on their options and choices made, and consider the subsequent outcomes in order to make better choices that value and respect everyone (DSC, 1996; Vance, 2015). In addition to providing children with opportunities to think about and discuss how they want to be as a class community, other topics that relate to interpersonal issues include rule making, decision making, and problem solving.

At the beginning of the school year, establishing classroom rules as a community helps to set behavioral expectations and consequences. Teachers who practice in democratic learning communities recognize children as decision-makers, guaranteeing them active voice and agency to help draft and implement class rules that everyone agrees are important to getting along and working together as a learning community.

Class meetings lead to dynamic dialogues, and TMaps provide the different metacognitive processes that can help to organize and facilitate learners' authentic voice and agency. The resulting cycle of authentic student voice and agency (https://youthadvocacy.us /family-supports-student-voice) ensures that all community members democratically (1) listen to everyone's ideas, (2) validate (acknowledge and appreciate) what everyone has to say, (3) authorize decision making through consensus (voting on recommendations), (4) act on the agreed-upon decisions, and (5) reflect on the decisions to determine whether they achieved the desired outcome (Figure 4.6).

In meetings (across life spans!), it is often difficult to pay attention as others speak because participants are busy internally processing their own

Figure 4.6. Cycle of Authentic Student Voice and Agency

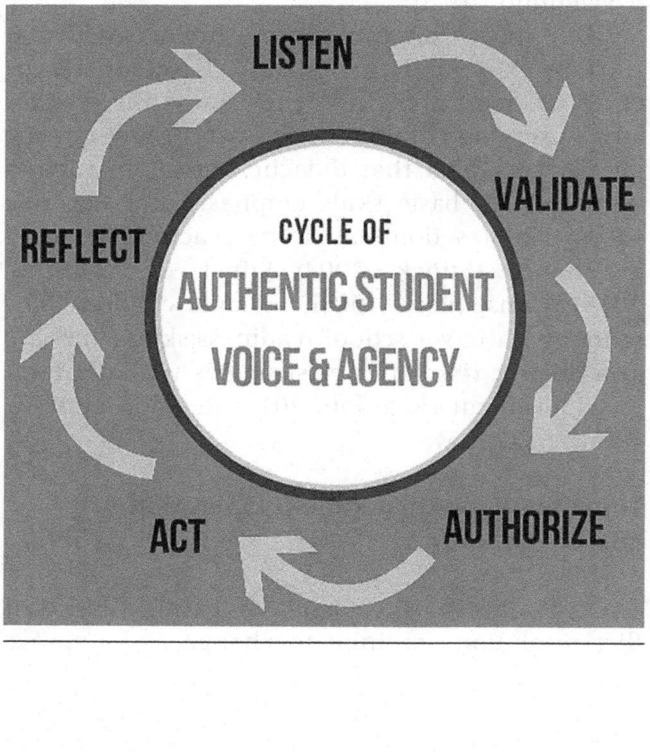

thoughts and interpretation simultaneously in anticipation of offering additional ideas and suggestions. TMaps, as visual representations that support spoken language, provide learners and teachers visual reference points (as all geographic maps do) for focusing attention on the patterns of thinking, not simply on isolated ideas.

Early in the school year, children can use TMaps to help identify and select rules that they want to emphasize as important reminders for how they want to operate (including conduct and behavior) as a community. For example, the classroom teacher can use a large floor Tree Map to help group important rules in relation to the class schedule and routines, or a Tree Map generated on the computer about the rules that apply to different locations at school (Figure 4.7).

This can be done inductively or deductively, and in highly generative ways by seeing new links and categories develop as ideas are drawn out in TMaps. Again, a Frame may be drawn around the Tree Map in order to highlight each learners' background Frame of Reference for rules. Learners can discuss how the rules they learn at home may differ from those created in the classroom.

Children can help negotiate and develop rules they feel are essential to completing daily tasks without disrupting or interfering with classmates' work. For example, rules for sharpening your pencil; lining up to go to lunch, recess, or specials; checking out books from the library; working at the computer station; walking in the hallways; selecting activities during free time; and getting ready to go home.

Once completed, the class can transfer the rules onto large chart paper and post them on the walls around the classroom. If issues or concerns emerge regarding any individual rules, children can discuss them during the daily class meetings. Children's voice and agency during TMap and other daily

learning activities empower children as leaders within their learning community.

Thinking Maps Promote Conflict Resolution. As noted by DeVries and Zan (2012), in classroom settings that encourage active social interaction, conflicts are inevitable. Rather than view conflict as undesirable and strive to avoid or eliminate it, see conflict as having practical and developmental value for learners and educators working cooperatively within group arrangements. As a framework that can institutionalize and connect theory to practice within inclusive settings (Hyerle, 1996), Thinking Maps metacognitively support conflict resolution during class meetings by helping children to structure, organize, discuss, and resolve the conflicts they encounter.

In particular, but not exclusively, the Multi-Flow Map has been used effectively by teachers, mediators, counselors, and learners to show the rising tension, as well as short- and long-term ripple effects of conflict. Flow Maps show visually how actions bring consequences, sometimes including unforeseen events and turning points that could have been averted if alternative actions had been taken. Facilitating predictive, cause-and-effect reasoning for showing repeating pattern responses (positive and negative) is essential to understanding conflicts and resolutions.

According to constructivist theory, conflict has two forms: interpersonal and intrapersonal. Intrapersonal conflict is internalized, often in the form of a contradiction between expectation and result (disequilibrium) and can lead to making new and more complex mental relationships. For example, a child who believes that whales are fish and becomes angry when contradicted must examine the available evidence in order to resolve her internal conflict as she forms new, complex mental relationships about whales using a variety of Thinking Maps, as described in Chapter 2.

On the other hand, interpersonal conflict occurs between or among individuals and can thus promote moral as well as intellectual development (Piaget, 1932/1965). After all, "social life," according to Piaget, "is a necessary condition for the development of logic" (p. 80). Higher-order interpersonal reasoning and logic takes place when children experience how others react to the feelings, ideas, and desires they share. When two or more children

Figure 4.7. Tree Map: Classifying Rules According to Location

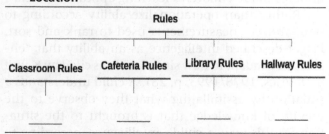

experience a conflict, they must develop higher-level interpersonal understanding as they increase their consciousness of others and their perspectives in relation to their own.

Interpersonal conflicts, such as two children wanting to use the stapler at the same time in the art center, can be broached during a class meeting. For example, the teacher and children could use a Double-Bubble Map to compare and contrast the two perspectives of what happened; a Flow Map to help document the series of events; and a Multi-flow Map to help depict what was said, what happened as a result, and possible solutions to help resolve the conflict. Using TMaps during conflict resolution helps children to *see* each other's thinking, and in the process helps to diffuse an emotionally charged conflict toward multiple visual pathways to an agreed-upon resolution. It is not uncommon for the same conflict resolutions to become newly adopted class rules.

Teaching to the Full Range of Learners

Children cannot learn membership apart from being a group member (Kliewer, 1998). Dynamic social contexts and activities in which no child is excluded, and all members' participation and contributions are encouraged and valued, foster and promote cognition and learning (Siegel, 2001). Helping children accept and appreciate multiple perspectives promotes a more collaborative than competitive learning environment.

While classification systems are created to ensure that learners receive individual services needed to be successful, especially within inclusive settings, this can simultaneously place additional demands on teachers who may lack adequate preparation to meet the unique needs of learners using differentiated supports. A major focus of this book is to help teachers implement Thinking Maps with the full range of young children within diverse, inclusive, democratic learning communities. For this reason, the construct of "regular" is not used, as it implies a dichotomy of "regular vs. irregular" that is neither accurate nor helpful.

Since learning and development is an individual matter, teachers anticipate and expect diversity in academic performance across any group of learners. This enables teachers to positively, proactively, and productively find ways to capitalize on children's varied talents and skills along the distribution of learning and development. The idea is to celebrate each child's uniqueness, no matter where they happen to fall along the developmental continuum, and to help each child move forward rather than rank and sort them into a vertical view of assumed deficit.

This is not to say that the children with multiple disabilities or intellectual disabilities who receive less than 40% of their instructional time in inclusive settings (Office of Special Education, 2018) would not benefit from TMap activities within non-inclusive settings. Children will certainly reap benefits in any setting or instructional group arrangement, inclusive or not. However, heterogenous instructional groups with varied learning and development tend to broaden and enrich children's participation into a more dynamic learning experience than what can otherwise be achieved within non-inclusive, homogeneous settings.

Thinking Maps Reveal All Children's Gifts and Talents

Psychological testing and assessment with racial/ethnic minority groups have been plagued with erroneous assumptions that these tests were objective, culture-free, and generalizable even though they were standardized, validated, and determined reliable primarily with White, middle-class, English-language populations (Olmedo, 1981; Reynolds, 1982). The accuracy and fair depiction of children's aptitude and potential are highly questionable and may result in lowered expectations and incorrect, invalid labels and placements, with underrepresentation in gifted programs (Grissom & Redding, 2016) and overrepresentation in special education (Camera, 2017). It has been suggested that Black students are underrepresented in gifted programs by 50 to 70% (Ford & Grantham, 2003). When children struggle academically, it is very easy for teachers to underestimate children's learning aptitude as well.

Rather than operationalize ability according to standardized measurements used to rank and sort, Piaget described intelligence as an ability that "enables us to adapt to new situations" (as cited by Kamii & DeVries, 1978/1993, p. 28). A child understands a situation by assimilating what they observe to the totality of knowledge that is brought to the situation. In this way, a child's intelligence, according to

Piaget (1971, 1981), organizes the world as it organizes itself. To maximize children's intelligence, we must maximize the quality of opportunities they experience. TMaps are uniquely Piagetian as they were designed as consistent, highly flexible, interdependent, transferrable, and developmental, as each learner "organizes" the world while grounded in eight patterns of thinking and embedded reflectiveness by using the Frame of Reference.

All children are encouraged to demonstrate their full potential, interests, and talents during creative map activities. Increased learner motivation combined with higher teacher expectations for all learners translate into improved academic outcomes. As children refine and strengthen their metacognitive processing, the complexity in their thoughts and communications across content areas deepens as well.

Thinking Maps Benefit All Language Learners. All young children are language learners. All children, including Dual Language Learners (DLLs), require meaningful language-based learning opportunities immersed within a flexible social atmosphere promoted by Thinking Maps. The eight metacognitive maps provide an important framework that help DLLs (and all learners) to actively construct mental relationships and form linguistic connections between concepts (schema of understanding), represented and expressed both visually and verbally. As children hear and use vocabulary and grammar (parts of speech) during TMap activities (eight cognitive processes), they expand their expressive and receptive vocabulary, meaning, and word usage as they make sense of the concepts learned and discussed.

Connecting home and school communities is an assets-based approach that capitalizes on the knowledge that is familiar to children, and upon which increasingly complex content-based learning is expanded (Civil, 2018). Incorporating children's cultural backgrounds and experiences (frames of reference) can be particularly helpful and beneficial, especially for children like DLLs, whose culture is different from the dominant culture. The various forms of expertise and practices developed and used within their homes and communities (funds of knowledge) can be strategically leveraged to promote learning (Llopart & Esteban-Guitart, 2018) during TMaps.

Parents can likewise use Thinking Maps at home to make decisions and considerations with regard to their daily routines and activities. Family conversations naturally tap into their cultural traditions, practices, experiences, values, and beliefs that comprise their funds of knowledge. To help parents and children develop weekly breakfast menus collaboratively, families can use a Circle Map to brainstorm possible menu items, such as eggs, waffles, pancakes, and pizza (Figures 4.8 and 4.9).

All learners can arguably prosper from language-rich activities within diverse, inclusive settings that guarantee every child full community membership. Multilingual learners in particular benefit from targeted small-group instruction using supporting materials that connect to daily content instruction (Castro et al., 2011; O'Connor et al., 2010, 2013). TMap activities readily capitalize on vocabulary and listening comprehension with early reading skills. When these important experiences begin in kindergarten, the proportion of children requiring assistance in later grades decreases (Connor et al., 2014; O'Connor et al., 2013). As an effective UDL experience, TMaps fully utilize children's first language, a proven aspect that helps support English-language skill acquisition and development (Castro et al., 2011). Children's excitement and eagerness to share their thoughts, ideas, and opinions during map activities is motivating for all learners, including children with disabilities.

Thinking Maps Benefit All Ability Learners. Perhaps no group of children is more varied, broad, or diverse than the subgroup containing children with disabilities. For young children ages 3 to 8, this group generally includes children with developmental delays in one or more developmental areas (cognitive, communication, social, emotional, or adaptive domains). The diverse differences across disabilities (e.g., Down syndrome, blindness, autism, cerebral palsy); the complexity of what happens when children have multiple disabilities (such as having a hearing impairment combined with Down syndrome); and what each means in terms of learning and instruction practice must be considered, while overgeneralizations must be avoided. Black children have been historically vulnerable for special education placement. While Black students are underrepresented in gifted education programs,

Figures 4.8 and 4.9. Circle Map: Brainstorming Breakfast Menu Items

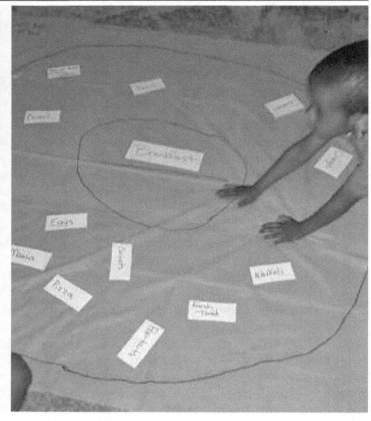

they tend to be disproportionately represented in lower-end special education placements (Proctor et al., 2012).

Teachers must consider individual children's strengths and areas needing improvement, impairments, medical conditions, and type of disability when planning instruction that will most likely entice their interest and participation. TMap activities with durable maps (plastic, vinyl, or taped diagrams on walls or floors) and real-world materials are generally emphasized for *all* young children. Durable maps allow for repeated practice, and familiar objects help to tap directly into children's funds of knowledge.

Observation, as noted in Chapter 3, plays a central role throughout the Inquiry Teaching Process. Observations over time reveal individual learner's demeanors, dispositions, temperaments, and personalities. Children who are shy, apprehensive, reluctant to take risks, or who experience tactile defensiveness or require additional time to orient

themselves spatially and physically within grouping arrangements may require extensive and repeated opportunities to work with small and large maps and materials.

Children who are less self-confident to voice their ideas publicly during map discussions may want to write down, draw, or verbalize their ideas into a tape recorder. Once all learners are afforded the adequate time needed to process and construct mental relationships and possible solutions, documented ideas can then be shared and discussed altogether as a group.

Scaffolding Learning and Zone of Proximal Development

Learning for all children begins at the zone of proximal development (ZPD). Vygotsky's best-known concept, ZPD is conceptualized as the space between what a child can do independently and what the child is capable of doing with support. Based largely on observations, teachers determine the extent to which a child can complete map activities across group settings. These observations denote the complexity of concepts and ideas in order to determine when to assist or intervene, as described in Chapter 3.

It is important for teachers to scaffold (assist) children's metacognitive processing, empowering the child to eventually complete maps as independently as possible. Productive questioning, as illustrated in Chapter 3, is one form of assistance that teachers use to scaffold young children's thinking and understanding. However, it is equally imperative to keep scaffolding to a minimum in order to avoid interfering with the child's agenda, ideas, reasoning, and problem solving. While some scaffolded assistance is intentionally reduced as children's skill development and understanding increases, productive questioning is not reduced nor eliminated but remains an integral means for guiding and facilitating the inquiry process.

Equity, Accessibility, and Universal Design Learning (UDL)

In order for *all* learners to gain access to, fully participate in, and achieve maximum profit from the eight metacognitive strategies, educators must understand, believe in, and value metacognitive strategies using the maps as a learning experience for *all children*. Valuing metacognition as important thinking processes that can be used by all children requires educators to view all children as capable of *metacognitive processing*.

Since 1990, when TMaps became available through in-depth professional development training across whole schools, the primary focus of the work with teachers has been an emphasis on developing independent fluency within all learners. An autobiographical activity titled "My Story" (Hyerle, 1990) is used as the primary introduction, over an 8-week time span. Every child learns each of the eight TMaps and Frame of Reference by using the content they know the most about—themselves! At the end of 8 weeks, every child has drawn eight maps about themself using blank sheets of paper. This further empowers them to "own" the TMaps as a language for learning content and to learn deeply about themselves.

"An accessible curriculum," according to the Division of Early Childhood (DEC), is one in which

"all aspects of the curriculum (e.g., environment, activities, materials) invite active participation of all children, regardless of disability or special needs" (2007, p. 4). An effective UDL curriculum, as recommended by Rose and Meyer (2002), provides flexible, customizable, child-centered, child-directed activities that are highly accessible to all learners.

This flexible metacognitive teaching and learning allows teachers and children to employ the metacognitive maps before, during, and after instruction across the content areas. The maps are easily customizable in size, color, and material, as detailed in Chapter 1. The implementation of tangible maps with movable objects, labels, and photos serves to increase the hands-on, three-dimensional nature of the mapping experience. These materials further stimulate and appeal to learners' visual–spatial, tactile, and kinesthetic learning modalities that are foundational to the full range of young children's learning experiences.

As a child-centered, child-directed approach, TMaps actively encourage children to voice their funds of knowledge and exercise their agency as they ask questions, brainstorm, take perspective, and problem-solve together. As a UDL approach, its effectiveness requires the application of differentiated instruction with appropriate accommodations and modifications as needed.

Differentiated Instruction—Accommodations and Modifications

Equal opportunity refers to every child's access to full and active participation in learning activities. Equity recognizes that in order for each child to reach an equal outcome (or to the fullest extent possible), needed resources and supports must be allocated including instructional accommodations and modifications.

Accommodations are the individualized changes or adjustments made to specific maps or map activities in order to maximize children's access, participation, and outcomes. Possible accommodations include altering or varying map materials, allowing children to use various response formats (including augmentative and alternative communication systems), and varying the physical arrangement (including individual, pair-share, small and large groups) within the learning environment.

Similar to accommodations, modifications to practices and expectations are also determined individually to support the different learning strengths and needs of diverse learners. Possible modifications include changes in the instructional level, content, and performance criteria, as well as varying assessment procedures and using alternative assessments. Altogether, UDL with differentiated instruction based on accommodation and modifications create an all-inclusive learning experience for everyone.

Teachers can easily create short teaching episodes (mini-lessons) and learning skills instruction, embedding learning objectives identified on young children's individualized family service plans (IFSPs), individualized education programs (IEPs), or intervention plans for DLLs directly into map activities. The following discussion outlines possible accommodations to address a range of learning and developmental considerations across developmental domains using Thinking Maps.

Accommodating Cognitive Considerations.
Children experiencing cognitive delays or learning challenges often have difficulties with cognitive processing (including metacognition) and executive functions (cognitive flexibility, working memory, and inhibitory control) that are key to academic learning. To accommodate learners during TMap activities, teachers can

- Use cues such as gestures (e.g., pointing, nodding), prompts, questions, or pictures.
- Use descriptive talk or Think Alouds to help the child attend to, and think about the concept learned using a specific metacognitive process. Think Alouds tap into metacognitive process by saying out loud possible reasoning and problem solving that help the child reflect, think, and apply it to the concept.
- Utilize competent, carefully selected mature peer mediators with the best disposition needed to help demonstrate, describe, and explain their completed map to the child with cognitive needs.

Utilizing advanced peers as mediators or peer supports is a nonthreatening, non-intrusive way to promote young children's active participation, interest, and motivation during TMap activities.

Accommodating Language and Communication Considerations.
More young children qualify for language-related services than any other developmental domain. Open-ended questions (as illustrated in Chapter 3) encourage and challenge children to respond beyond simple yes/no answers. To further support children's communication as children engage with TMaps, teachers can

- Sit in front of the child, face to face, and model this strategy for peer supports.
- Use descriptive talk and Think Alouds to help encourage receptive and expressive language development.
- Comment on or repeat children's statements with additional vocabulary and information.
- Collaborate with Speech and Language Pathologists to help address speech fluency, vocabulary development, and articulation goals using TMaps.

Accommodating Fine and Gross Motor Considerations.
Children experiencing fine or gross motor delays may have differences in their ability to use joints, bones, or muscles due to contributing medical conditions such as cerebral palsy, spina bifida, or muscular dystrophy. Physical or occupational therapists should be consulted for specialized support services and appropriate use of adaptive equipment. To accommodate fine and gross motor considerations, teachers can

- Provide ample time and physical space for completing individual and group map activities.
- Use Rubbermaid shelving liner, Velcro, or other non-slip material as needed to help stabilize materials on maps.
- Allow children to create individual maps using rulers and stencils to draw lines and shapes. Children can glue on circles, rectangles, and squares and use yarn or chenille wire to help form the different map diagrams as well.

- Provide children with mobility items such as a toy shopping cart to collect and transport materials.
- Use adaptive positioning items to support children's posture (stabilized and supported trunk) and free the child's hands to reach, hold, or handle materials.
- Use correctly sized adapted chairs to allow the child's feet to rest flat on the floor or on an elevated footrest.

Fine and perceptual motor development is encouraged as children grasp and position items on maps or use scissors, glue, and writing tools (using a pincer grip) to create their own maps.

Accommodating Social and Emotional Considerations. Children who are less flexible, tolerant, or become easily agitated, struggling with self-regulation and inhibitory control, can experience social rejection from peers that further impedes or hinders their social (and communication) development. TMaps create inviting, warm, and noncompetitive contexts for establishing working relationships and friendships as young children collaborate and cooperate, actively taking turns and sharing materials. To further promote social skills, teachers can

- Maintain a regular TMap routine/schedule to increase children's familiarity and sense of security.
- Create varied workspaces that allow for cooperative small- and large-group participation and quiet workspaces that allow for independent mapping.
- Use peer supports to help model appropriate social behaviors (quiet indoor voice; using words to express wants, needs, and emotions; the proper way to carry and handle materials).

CONCLUSION

The active engagement and socialization that takes place during TMaps makes them ideal instructional tools during class meetings and the conflict resolution process, especially within democratic learning communities. As children work collaboratively using TMaps to learn academic content, create class rules, or find resolutions to conflicts, every child must be granted full participation as valued community members. This means that each child has equal opportunity to exercise their voice and agency as they help to complete large group TMaps, openly expressing their thoughts, ideas, and diverse perspectives while freely responding to others.

The purpose of this chapter is to illustrate that *all children* can engage in high-quality, universally designed early metacognitive activities. All children must be guaranteed universal access to, and participation in, map activities. To achieve this goal, educators must recognize, emphasize, and satisfy each child's individual uniqueness along the continuum of learning and development.

General accommodations are recommended to foster and maximize diverse learner's skill acquisition, learning, and development across developmental domains and academic content areas during TMap activities. However, teachers are cautioned against making overgeneralizations. Outcomes will invariably be different because learners are undeniably different. TMap activities cannot promise identical learning and developmental outcomes in general and gains in metacognitive processing and understanding and academic content knowledge specifically. An emphasis on what is educationally relevant and personally respectful to young children along a continuum of development can increase the likelihood that individual achievement will be maximized using Thinking Maps.

CHAPTER 5

Thinking Maps Provide Authentic Formative Assessment and Documentation

Kindergarten teachers taking down centers (blocks, housekeeping); limiting social and communication skills; limiting building experiences and talking about it; less problem solving; and more seatwork. Recess trend is that a lot of schools NOT allowed anymore—NO recess after lunch at a lot of schools. There are developmental repercussions for no recess/outdoor play. All learn same thing at same time and penalize anyone for not knowing . . . Fear of our school receiving a bad grade. Fear of not getting a salary increase. Fear in children failing a test. Fear of being retained. There's a lot of fear! That's not what education is about. That's the ANTITHESIS of education! (Counsell, 2007, pp. 255–256).

The kinds of high-quality learning opportunities that can best promote 21st-century content and skills, such as deep learning, critical thinking, problem solving, communication, and collaboration, as discussed in Chapter 3, require accountability systems that reflect these ambitious academic standards and achievement goals. Rather than subjugate children, teachers, and schools to more compliance and efforts to avoid punitive consequences (Center for American Progress and the Council of Chief State School Officers, 2014; Darling-Hammond et al., 2014), educators, scholars, and reform advocates propose school accountability that promotes flexible, continuous support and improvement with ongoing evaluation and self-reflection (Darling-Hammond & Plank, 2015).

This chapter begins with a brief historical perspective of high-stakes standardized testing in the United States and the negative consequences for learners, especially children from historically marginalized

groups. Rather than rely on singular test scores in content areas such as English Language Arts or math, a holistic approach is recommended using multiple measures that more accurately reveal the individual strengths, interests, and needs of children and communities. This important conversation will include a discussion about how to use Thinking Maps as authentic, formative permanent products that help assess children's content knowledge and understanding in addition to documenting their effective use of the eight metacognitive process strategies to aid and support their own learning and development.

A BRIEF HISTORICAL PERSPECTIVE OF STANDARDIZED TESTING

Standardized testing has a longstanding history in the nation's schools and classroom practices (Counsell, 2007; Reese, 2013; Walker, 2017). Standardized tests have been controversial from the outset, with their origins in the Eugenics movement. Psychological tests and assessments were developed according to Eugenics beliefs that differences in intelligence, aptitude, and other abilities not only exist among individuals but can be attributed to their genes, race, and ethnicity and objectively quantified to reveal which groups are superior and inferior (Selden, 2000; Singham, 1995).

Inferiority/Pathology Model and Cultural Deprivation Model

Since the majority of intelligence and aptitude tests were standardized, validated, and determined reliable primarily with White, middle-class, English-language populations, these assessments are not objective, culture-free, or generalizable to other racial/ethnic groups. Standardized assessment biases result in lower test scores for minority groups and, in turn, are used as evidence to assert their genetic and biological deficiency, referred to as the Inferiority/Pathology Model.

The Inferiority/Pathology Model was later replaced with the Cultural Deprivation Model. This model is used to blame lower test scores on the cultural beliefs, values, and practices of minority groups. Both models have been scrutinized for their racist ideology and cultural insensitivity, largely and overtly contributing to the ongoing marginalization of minority students in public education (Leong & Park, 2016; Reynolds, 1982).

As a prominent model for educational reform, the Standards Movement is comprised of three key policy components: (1) rigorous standards in core subject areas, (2) tests aligned with these standards, and (3) accountability for results. High-stakes accountability systems use standardized test scores to rank and sort children (and schools) into vertical hierarchies of high and low performers with a continued overrepresentation of achievement gaps falling along historically marginalized socioeconomic and racial groups. The subsequent reform initiatives, including the No Child Left Behind Act of 2001, the Race to the Top Initiative of 2009, and the Common Core Curriculum Initiative of 2008/2013 linked standards and test scores with accountability. Yet all three initiatives ultimately failed to address how the dynamics of human performance are influenced by pedagogy, hegemony, and expectations (Washington et al., 2016).

Research has further revealed significant concerns regarding the impact that ranking and sorting mechanisms have on schools, learning, classroom practice, teachers, and learners (e.g., Counsell, 2007; Nichols et al., 2006, 2012; Walker, 2017). As elaborated passionately in the testimonial noted earlier, the teacher at an inner-city school in Florida made the painful decision to leave kindergarten after a 32-year career in protest against the negative impact of high-stakes testing on teachers, children, curriculum, and practice (Counsell, 2007). The urgency to raise test scores at her school resulted in curriculum and practices that were not

developmentally appropriate, culturally sensitive, or responsive to individual learning strengths and needs (e.g., more skill-drill isolated facts and worksheets; teacher-directed lecture; no outdoor recess; no child-directed center time).

Culturally Different Model

The movement toward cultural sensitivity has resulted in the Culturally Different Model, replacing the previous racist, deficit models used to explain test score differences. Rather than interpret differences between Whites and minorities as indicating pathology or inferiority, differences are no longer misinterpreted as deficiencies but are rather understood as just what they are—mere differences (Leong & Park, 2016).

As cultural beings, all humans possess values, assumptions, biases, and cultural experiences. The notion that the backgrounds of test designers (who are predominantly White Americans who reflect White American values) influence the design of intelligence tests is unavoidable (Washington et al., 2016). Assessment measures are therefore created ethnocentrically by test designers, which inevitably results in test bias and discrimination for individuals who belong to other cultures. Hence, it is near impossible to develop a singular test that is "universally applicable or equally fair to all cultures" (Anastasi & Urbina, 1997, p, 342).

Ranking and sorting children using biased and discriminatory measures leading to deficit views of aptitude and achievement must be abandoned in favor of multiple assessments that in combination, can more accurately capture and holistically depict children's learning and developmental strengths, interests, and needs. Understanding and appreciating that all children fall along a continuum of learning and development places a greater emphasis on assessing where individual learners are in their learning trajectory and designing curricula and instruction to best promote learner outcomes. In this regard, TMaps can provide meaningful data to help establish what children know, what they can do, and how well they understand and apply each metacognitive strategy.

A key to the added value of TMaps for assessment purposes is that it is a coherent, universal model of eight fundamental cognitive processes that integrate verbal, visual, spatial, and kinesthetic representations, thus expanding the access to learners across modalities, and cognitive styles. In addition, because TMaps are integrated into the entire classroom experience and across content disciplines, this language for learning is what has been defined as "bifocal assessment" for revealing the content knowledge above, along with the deeper thinking patterns below (Hyerle & Williams, 2011).

CLASSROOM ASSESSMENTS

As a process, assessment entails the collection, documentation, organization, and interpretation of evidence based on children's learning and development from multiple sources. As a means, assessment refers to any type of measurement and appraisal of what children know and can demonstrate. Possible assessments include tests, observations, interviews, and reports. Ideally, multiple sources of evidence are collected at different times, in different contexts, and sometimes by different professionals and then recorded, integrated, and interpreted by qualified individuals who are sensitive to individual learners (Russell & Airasian, 2011).

Teachers use a variety of classroom assessments to help identify and document a child's strengths, needs, and progress. The information gathered is then used to guide and inform instructional practices and curricular decisions to best support and maximize learner outcomes.

Performance-Based Assessments

Performance-based assessments help teachers either to determine which children demonstrate a particular skill or to create a product to show their learning (Chappuis et al., 2011). Most performance-based assessments are authentically administered as part of children's daily life, routines, and learning (such as tying their shoes) within settings where they are naturally occurring.

Performance-based assessments can be used formatively and summatively. Formative assessments are imbedded within the teaching–learning process, helping to shape and improve individualized instruction. This means that children do not stop and drop what they are doing in order to be assessed but,

rather, teachers assess as they participate in learning activities. In this way, children are often not fully aware they are being assessed, eliminating the stress and anxiety they might experience with a conventional test. The removal of test anxiety further serves to increase the likelihood that children will perform at their highest level.

Summative assessments help to document learning gains and program effectiveness at the end of a unit of study. Children can write and read reports or create a poster with illustrations as a final assessment. The most effective teachers appraise children's learning and development on an ongoing basis and make the necessary revisions to their instructional practices and interactions accordingly.

Before and After Learning and Instruction

As discussed in Chapter 3, TMaps can be implemented and used to help document and assess learning throughout the teaching–learning process with any unit of study across content areas. Throughout the Inquiry Teaching Model (ITM), observation is a major source of information used to guide and facilitate children's learning. Much like the widely used K-W-L, the Circle Map is recommended for use at the outset or introduction of any unit of study or to help engage children's interest and curiosity according to the ITM. As children brainstorm using the Circle Map or describe the topic using adjectives with the Bubble Map, teachers can determine and document children's prior knowledge and understanding needed to guide and inform their instruction.

For example, an introduction to a unit of study about U.S. currency as a medium of exchange for goods and services with young children can focus specifically on money. Beginning with coins and then learning about the different dollar amounts, a teacher can place the word "money," pictures, and fake or real money in the center of the Circle Map. Children brainstorm everything they know about money, including the different coins and bills; how they receive it (e.g., tooth fairy, birthday, allowance, house chores, mowing yards, shoveling sidewalks, lemonade stands); where they keep it (e.g., billfolds, purses, piggybanks, bank accounts); where they spend it (e.g., grocery store, post office, restaurant, auto shop, beauty salon, dentist office); and what they like to purchase (e.g., treats, clothes, toys, games, sports, hobbies, music, movies). A Circle Map can also be used to brainstorm how many combinations of coins can be used to represent a specific amount such as a one dollar bill, as demonstrated in a bilingual classroom (Figure 5.1).

Here we see the rectangular Frame of Reference added to encourage learners to reflect on how they know (their existing funds of knowledge) and have learned about money from different sources of information (such as a math book).

Children can then work independently to describe individual coins using a Bubble Map as a pre-assessment to determine how much they know at the outset of the study unit. All of the completed Bubble Maps can then be compared and discussed during whole-group instruction, allowing children to ask questions and to check for understanding.

Toward the end of the unit of study, children can complete individual Tree Maps to classify coins as they compare and contrast what they knew about U.S. coins at the beginning of the study and what they now know and understand (learned) at the end of the study (Figure 5.2). To make sure children haven't simply memorized isolated facts about U.S. coins, they can complete post-assessments individually by applying their knowledge to complete other TMaps, such as using a Bridge Map to demonstrate the value of each U.S. coin (Figure 5.3). This is an example of a "bifocal assessment," as a teacher (and learners) may look at the content of the vocabulary and concepts; discuss the degree of effectiveness of the TMaps; and assess growth in their abilities to transfer thinking processes.

Permanent Products and Portfolios

Permanent products generally include real or concrete items or outcomes that result from a direct effort. In education, specifically, permanent products often take the form of creative projects, stories, drawings, sketches, posters, presentations, K-W-Ls, journals, tests, or quizzes. As described above, TMaps make ideal permanent products because they accurately capture and depict children's learning, understanding, and metacognition in real time throughout the inquiry teaching–learning process.

Portfolios in education are authentic sampling systems that provide an in-depth portrait that shows how a child works, including the character and

quality of that work (performance) over a duration of time that can easily be shared with parents. With so much time and effort that teachers devote to planning and actual instruction, it is imperative that the kinds of portfolio items or permanent products included in the child's portfolio are informative, easy to collect, and meaningful.

Four types of portfolios are broadly recognized: (1) Showcase, (2) Evaluation, (3) Documentation, and (4) Process. While there is some variation across the different types (such as the showcase portfolio, which is a collection of a children's best and/or favorite work), many class portfolios include a combination of permanent products in order to demonstrate a child's work and progress over time. For example, one unit of study that young children first encounter in preschool and continue to refine and expand on their ideas into the primary grades are the five senses. Children enjoy exploring items visually and auditorily as well as touching, smelling, and tasting items (when appropriate). Capitalizing on the five modalities during TMap activities with young children is central to our approach and application.

A class portfolio on the five senses could include a large Tree Map that classifies familiar items according to the five senses (Figure 5.4). Items can be placed in a bag and children take turns removing an item and placing it on the map. As a learning community, children may want to take a deeper dive into examining specific foods, such as apples. Children can learn about the parts of an apple, smelling and tasting as appropriate, using a Brace Map (Figures 5.5 and 5.6). After tasting three types of apples (e.g., red delicious, yellow delicious, and granny smith) children can vote on their favorite and graph the results as a group, determining the most popular choice (Figure 5.7).

Children can likewise complete Bridge Maps to demonstrate the association between which body part is used for each sense (Figure 5.8). All photos serve as digital documentation in the class portfolio. Once children correctly associate each body part with its corresponding sense, educators can use a large Multi-Flow Map to help them understand how the sensations they receive are sent to the brain for processing, such as the brain interpreting different colors perceived by our eyes (Figures 5.9 and 5.10).

While we do not advocate for fill-in-the-blank worksheets (Figure 5.11), individual TMaps can be

Figure 5.1. Circle Map: Brainstorming Different Amounts Equaling One Dollar

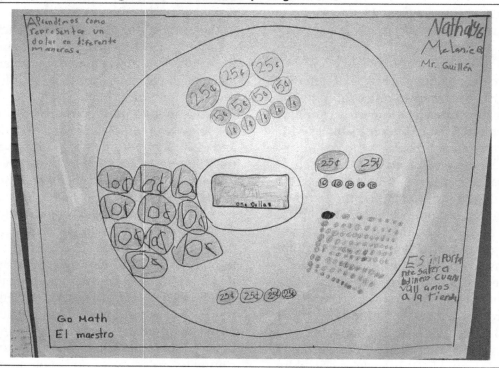

Figure 5.2. Tree Map: Classifying U.S. Coins

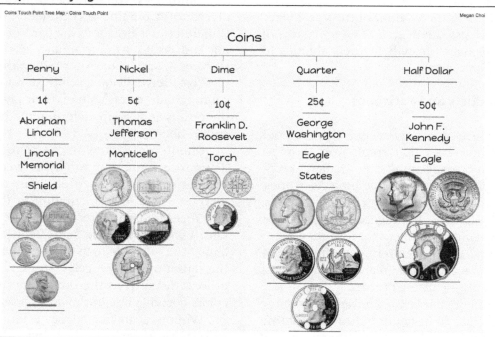

used as a post-assessment to document what children recall and understand, including a Double-Bubble Map comparing apples (Figure 5.12). A documentation board in the classroom can likewise showcase how children use their senses to describe other favorite foods, such as popcorn, as a group and individually (Figures 5.13 and 5.14). The more we tap into children's individual interests such as choosing their favorite foods to describe using the five senses, the greater their intrinsic motivation to think and write about that topic. TMap activities capitalize on individual preferences, perspectives, and prior experiences in

ways that are culturally responsive, allowing children to express their funds of knowledge, which further elevates learning in meaningful, purposeful, and relevant ways for them and their families.

Raw scores and percentages of correct items on a multiple-choice test are difficult to interpret and determine which items the child fully or partially mastered since it is not known whether the child guessed, got confused, or misread the question or

Figure 5.3. Bridge Map: Coin and Monetary Value Analogy

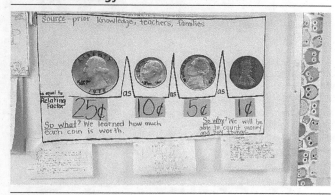

Figure 5.4. Tree Map: Classifying Items by the Five Senses

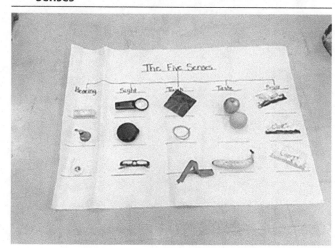

Figures 5.5 and 5.6. Brace Maps: Parts of an Apple

Photos courtesy of SWTCC Child Care Center—Union Campus.

Figure 5.7. Graphing Favorite Type of Apple Using Five Senses

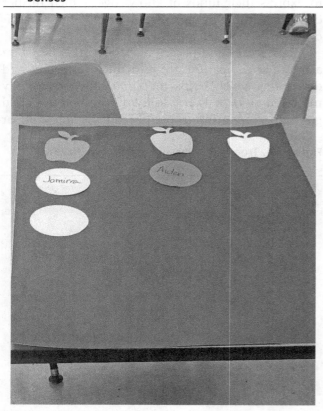

Figure 5.8. Bridge Map: Body Parts and Five Sense Analogies

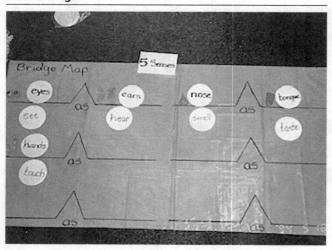

Figure 5.9. Multi-Flow Map: Cause–Effect Relationship Between Sensations and the Brain

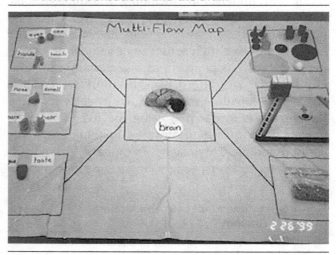

Figure 5.10. Multi-Flow Map: Cause–Effect Relationship Between Sensations and the Brain

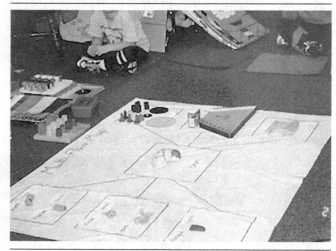

possible answers. As permanent products, TMaps allow parents and teachers to visualize what children know and understand in relation to specific content and concepts such as money. TMaps also reveal how

well children use each metacognitive process to help them make sense of, visually convey, and communicate what they know to others. In this way, TMaps provide direct and practical evidence of children's metacognitive processing skills *specifically*, which can only be inferred by other assessments (at best).

As an assessment tool, TMaps document the interaction taking place between a child's academic learning and metacognitive processing (bifocal assessment) that helps to further explain why children are experiencing areas of academic strengths and needs. With guidance and support from teachers and parents, children can then use the same TMaps

Figure 5.11. Bubble Map: Using Senses to Describe Apples

Figure 5.12. Double-Bubble Map: Comparing and Contrasting Apples

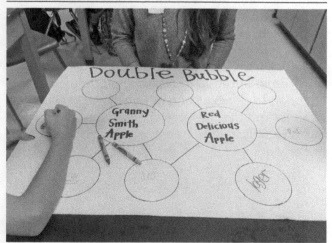

Figure 5.13. Bubble Map: Using Senses to Describe Popcorn (Whole Group)

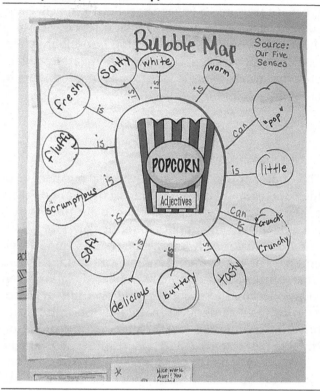

Figure 5.14. Bubble Map: Using Senses to Describe Popcorn (Individual)

as instructional tools at home to provide additional support and practice.

Over the long-term development of every learner's content knowledge, language, concepts, and skills, many children see learning as primarily about what they know, not how they know it, or even the influences on their prior knowledge. TMaps, as used throughout the teaching-learning-assessment cycle, offer the short-term benefit of immediate feedback on the learner's content knowledge and cognitive processes, but, perhaps more importantly, provide a long-term stance and explicit focus on self-assessment. We want learners to engage in reflective practice and come to determine and understand (even measure) their own growth as they develop into highly effective thinkers, problem solvers, and empathic, collaborative learners who also see the depth of thinking in others.

CONCLUSION

This chapter provided a brief historical perspective of high-stakes standardized testing in the United States as the critical backdrop to help explain their inherent and biased assumptions, particularly for children from historically marginalized and minoritized groups. The subsequent ranking and sorting system (that continues to dominate public education even today) declared test scores as the scientific evidence used to justify inferiority/pathology or cultural deprivation assumptions with subsequent distribution (tracking) of resources and opportunities accordingly.

A heavy reliance on singular test scores in content areas such as English Language Arts or math may not be accurate, with potentially devastating high-stakes consequences such as grade retention and increased dropout rates. Instead, a holistic approach is generally recommended in contemporary education, using multiple sources of qualitative data that more accurately reveal children's learning and developmental strengths, interests, and areas of need. As formative permanent products, TMaps provide the kind of high-quality, authentic evidence needed to demonstrate what children know and *how* they understand in real time.

In addition to assessing children's content knowledge and concept development, TMaps further demonstrate children's effective application of the eight metacognitive processes and Frame of Reference used to aid and support their own learning and development. As discussed in this chapter, examining "how" effectively children use their metacognitive processing to learn academic content and concepts can help to explain children's academic strengths and challenges. These gained insights can then be used by teachers and parents to better implement more effective interventions, such as TMaps, to increase children's academic performance by improving their metacognitive processing skills.

Throughout this book, we have detailed the learning and developmental benefits of using Thinking Maps. This discussion has outlined for teachers and parents how to best implement the TMaps to promote the full range of young children's (1) development across the different domains and (2) academic learning across content areas. While the learning and developmental benefits of using Thinking Maps with young children are evident, educators and parents must keep in mind that outcomes will vary across learners because each and every learner is undeniably unique.

TMap activities can promise neither identical learning and developmental outcomes in general, nor specific gains in metacognitive processing and understanding and academic content knowledge. We argue, instead, that what can be achieved using TMaps is greater—that is, more likely to maximize learner outcomes—than what could be accomplished without them. This will ultimately lead learning in the decades ahead to be less focused on the singular attention to testable content knowledge, shifting instead toward the full development of thinking, feeling, and reflection required to take positive actions in our world.

CHAPTER 6

The Science Underlying Thinking Maps With Young Children

There are 16 Habits of Mind that have proven key to unlocking students' attitudes about thinking and solving problems as well as improve their performance. These "habits" have been identified and refined by a colleague, Dr. Art Costa, and are based on decades of research and successful classroom practice. When we think about habits, we usually talk about incidental things we do, either good or bad. The same goes for thinking; there are good and bad habits that start when a child is a toddler (David Hyerle, personal communication, 2020).

RESEARCH AND THEORETICAL FOUNDATION FOR THINKING MAPS

As discussed extensively in Chapter 4, constructivist theory is based on the belief that young children actively construct knowledge and frameworks of understanding (cognitive schema of mental relationships) as they interpret their experiences in physical and social worlds. According to this view, knowledge is not transmitted but actively *constructed* by learners. Children internally construct cognitive schema as they act on objects and engage with people and activities.

Thinking Maps naturally complement and support the constructivist accommodation-assimilation process. As a visual model of interrelated cognitive processes, TMaps help learners visualize the mental patterns they use to make sense of their own stored knowledge in order to assimilate new information and concepts and further expand their schema of understanding. Children's intelligence, according to Piaget, organizes the world as it organizes itself (Piaget, 1971, 1981). The more children construct mental relationships, the more they increase their cognition, intellectual ability, and aptitude. As illustrated throughout this book, TMaps work to guide and facilitate children's meaningful and relevant construction of mental relationships and, in turn, help to maximize children's intellectual powers.

EXECUTIVE FUNCTION

Cognition refers to the mental functions involved in attention, thinking, understanding, learning, remembering, solving problems, and making decisions. "Cognition is a fundamental aspect of an individual's ability to engage in activities, accomplish goals, and successfully negotiate the world" (Institute of Medicine, 2015, p. 2). While cognition and memory are often oversimplified as synonymous, cognition is much more multidimensional, involving numerous interrelated abilities that depend on brain anatomy and physiology.

Executive function (EF) is a multidimensional construct (Meltzer, 2018; Raver & Blair, 2016; Zelazo et al., 2016) comprised of integrated core components and processes (i.e., working memory, cognitive flexibility, and inhibitory control) that develops throughout life, with rapid and significant development in preschool (Diamond, 2013; Rueda et al., 2012). Together, the core EF components enable higher-order skills such as reasoning, problem solving, and planning (McClelland et al., 2010). It has been theorized that EF elements are important kindergarten readiness skills that lead to social-emotional competence and later academic achievement (Rueda et al., 2012).

Moran and Gardner (2018) proposed that EF processes and skills generally progress through three stages. In the first stage, identified as the apprentice stage, skill development is experienced by all people. In this stage, learners primarily use EF strategies to stay on task. In stage two, the master stage, individuals use EF strategies to connect personal beliefs and experiences with cultural beliefs in order to achieve identified goals. In the final, contributor stage, EF strategies empower individuals to maintain the momentum on purposeful actions in order to guide, inform, and understand their own cultural development.

If classroom instruction is largely limited to teacher-centered, teacher-directed approaches (as noted in Chapter 4), it is less likely that children's EFs will progress beyond the apprentice stage of development. For this reason, Moran and Gardner suggest that teachers need to adopt roles as guides, coaches, and facilitators who use cooperative contribution-oriented learning experiences, like Thinking Maps, that free children to openly express their ideas, thoughts, opinions, and perspectives as they increasingly take responsibility for their own learning. As a learner-center model, TMaps are introduced at each stage of children's evolution in executive functioning to explicitly develop their metacognitive capacities.

Thinking Maps Promote Children's Working Memory

Working memory, guided by focused attention, enables children to simultaneously process and store new information, manipulating and updating information as they complete mental tasks that include problem solving and reasoning (Diamond & Ling, 2016; Gray et al., 2017; Meltzer, 2018). As children grow and learn over time, they engage in tasks that are increasingly demanding cognitively. Difficulties related to EF may be due to a child's struggles in one of the three components or a problem in integrating the three and effectively applying them during classroom activities and tasks.

A young child actively uses their working memory to successfully complete multistep tasks such as brushing their teeth or tying their shoes. If a child struggles with working memory, that could impede or interfere with the child's ability to store or manipulate information as the child completes multistep tasks, solves problems, thinks strategically, or

engages in any higher-order conceptual thinking (Rhodes et al., 2016; Swanson, 2011; Viterbori et al., 2015).

Young children need multiple and varied opportunities to develop EF skills through practice using dynamic learning materials like TMaps. TMap activities help to facilitate and support young children's working memory throughout the learning experience. For example, a Flow Map facilitates children's working memory as they sequence events, tasks, or processes. In literacy, children can easily sequence the events in stories (retelling stories) like *Brown Bear, Brown Bear, What Do You See?* by Bill Martin Jr.; *Froggy Gets Dressed* by Jonathan London; *If You Give a Mouse a Cookie* by Laura Numeroff; and *All Fall Down* by Brian Wildsmith (Figures 6.1 and 6.2). While the Story *All Fall Down* has a specific order, *Froggy Gets Dressed* follows a sequence that keeps changing as the character adds a forgotten piece of clothing. This allows for an engaging discussion around how individual children prefer to get dressed, and children can take turns sequencing the items, using their individual logic to explain their decision.

In addition to self-help life skills, such as learning to tie their shoes, children can likewise sequence the steps in a recipe (e.g., making pancakes) or the directions to a specified location, such as going to school (which includes the mathematical concepts of measurement, distance, directionality, and spatial

Figure 6.1. Flow Map: Sequencing the Children's Story *All Fall Down*

awareness), or scientific concepts such as an animal food chain or life cycle (e.g., an apple or a butterfly) (Figure 6.3).

In every instance, regardless of the concept or content skill being used and practiced, children are actively engaging their working memory as they complete the Flow Map. If a child is struggling with

Figure 6.2. Flow Map: Sequencing Clothing Items in *Froggy Gets Dressed*

remembering and sequencing concepts or skills like typing shoes, teachers can take photos of children as they complete each step in the process. Children can then use the still photos to place them in the correct order on the map to help them visualize the procedure/process that, in turn, further cues and supports their working memory.

Additionally, because the TMaps are used together in varied combinations, children begin to make connections among these processes that further improve working memory. As a child uses the Flow Map to order the steps used in tying shoes (supporting working memory), the child can simultaneously use the Brace Map to identify and name the part–whole relationships of the shoe or a Double-Bubble Map to compare and contrast the similarities and differences between tennis shoes with laces and tennis shoes with Velcro (both maps promote cognitive flexibility).

Thinking Maps Promote Children's Cognitive Flexibility

The EF component of cognitive flexibility refers to a child's ability to consider multiple ways (and perspectives) to solve problems (Zelazo et al., 2016) and to be able to adjust, as needed, to changing priorities or demands (Diamond & Ling, 2016). Cognitive flexibility is used by children whenever they "change their focus of attention or shift their behavior from one activity or set of rules to another" (Cameron, 2018, p. 27). TMaps encourage children's cognitive flexibility as they shift their focus and application from using one Thinking Map (cognitive process) and related set of facts and information to another.

Figure 6.3. Flow Map: Sequencing the Butterfly Life Cycle

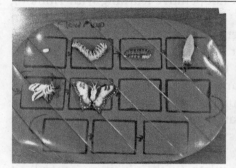 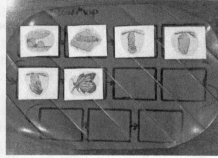 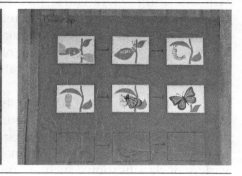

Similar to a Venn Diagram, the Double-Bubble Map enables children to compare (similarities) and contrast (differences) between two items or concepts, such as plants and animals. However, unlike the Venn, the Double-Bubble Map contains distinct graphic "bubbles" that further support and enhance children's visual discrimination and spatial awareness, enabling them to better focus and use their memory without distraction. As children identify what plants and animals have in common (shared traits such as both are living), they place objects, pictures, or words that represent the concepts or ideas in the center circles. As children identify differences, they place the objects, pictures, or words in the corresponding outer circles for plants and animals (see Figure 3.32 in Chapter 3).

As children identify the similarities and differences, they define, interpret, and elaborate what each item or concept means to them. Navigating and managing the criteria used to compare and contrast items and ideas helps children to develop and strengthen their cognitive flexibility.

Children's cognitive flexibility is further challenged and enhanced during classification activities. Children use Tree Maps to classify items into groups or categories according to similarities and differences. As children sort, group, and classify multiple items into categories based on similarities and differences, they use multiple characteristics and specific criteria to qualify and determine group membership. Tree Maps allow children to visualize the hierarchy and overall pattern of relationships that are not nearly as clearly and concisely captured and expressed in the typical descriptions provided by teachers. Verbal conversations are supported and enriched visually with complementary TMaps, along with the use of manipulatives, that gives children the added benefit of seeing how scholars form hierarchies (taxonomies). Later, however, as concepts become increasingly difficult to show with hands-on manipulatives, learners are left with verbal descriptions of classifications that have multiple levels of generality, with lots of details.

Science, as noted in Chapter 3, is a content area with several classifications that young children can use to help them make sense of their world and surroundings. Children can sort animal models into a variety of classifications, such as animals born alive versus animals that hatch from eggs, as illustrated in Chapter 3 (see Figure 3.24).

The more complex the classifications, the more children are challenged to use their cognitive flexibility as they consider multiple and intersecting criteria. While birds and mammals both care for their young (a shared trait), for example, only mammals have mammary glands to feed their young milk. In sum, the different ways items may be classified are directly supported by the other processes and patterns of TMaps, namely, by traits using a Bubble Map, by similar context using a Circle Map, and by physiology using a Flow Map.

SELF-REGULATION

Executive function (generally) and inhibitory control (specifically) contribute significantly to a child's ability to fully develop self-regulation. Self-regulation is a broader construct than EF, encompassing the ability to cope and adapt to outside stimuli and changing conditions that range from reactive processes like temperament to reflective and deliberate EF processes (Cameron, 2018). While all children have the capacity for self-regulation, not all self-regulation involves the deliberate and thoughtful choices that define EF, such as an infant sucking on a pacifier to help cope with a bombardment of unfamiliar voices and faces in a busy environment like a store. In classroom settings, children need to be able to integrate the different EF components in order to thrive and learn.

As children work cooperatively in pairs, small groups, or large-group settings to complete TMap activities, they simultaneously tap into their inhibitory control as they self-regulate their attention (focus), behavior (action), and emotions in order to fully participate. Cooperative learning with Thinking Maps (like the whole-group activity described in the chapter-opening vignette) encourages children to regulate their attention, emotions, and actions as they take turns to openly share and eagerly brainstorm ideas; learn to respectfully consider, discuss, and debate multiple perspectives; and negotiate, problem-solve, and make decisions in order to reach group consensus (see Chapter 4).

With young children who are developing their ability to self-regulate (with inhibitory control), it may be necessary to first begin implementing TMaps in whole-group settings, often during circle time or class meetings, as described throughout this book. Whole-group arrangements allow teachers to use productive questions (see Chapter 3) and dialoguing to help children focus, engage, and moderate their excitement and interest as they practice using the different maps and related cognitive processes. As children's self-regulation increases, so does their confidence and independence with using the various TMaps individually, in pairs, and in small groups.

The TMap formats promoted in this book for use with young children (ages 3–8) are three-dimensional, using actual tactile objects, photos, or drawings that children can grasp, see, and physically place on either large or small colorful vinyl TMaps (see Chapter 1). Actual objects and photos help young children symbolize/represent their ideas and concepts that are meaningful, purposeful, and relevant to them as they make sense of academic content, skills, the classroom environment, and learning opportunities experienced. The more young children practice self-regulation during TMap activities, the greater the likelihood they will increase their confidence, interest, and motivation to learn. Increased confidence leads to increased success and learning, a circular relationship that becomes a self-fulfilling prophecy of "I can!"

HABITS OF MIND

Just as Thinking Maps provide young children with important opportunities to fully utilize their EF skills, TMaps also encourage the development of the habits of mind (or dispositions) that support general decision making. Closely related to—and intersecting with—EF skills, Hyerle (2000) grouped (classified) the 12 habits of mind (which have more recently been updated to include 16 habits [Costa, 1999; Costa & Kallick, 2000]) according to three types of visual tools: (1) Thinking (Process) Maps, (2) Graphic Organizers, and (3) Brainstorm Webbing.

For the purpose of this book, the focus on Thinking Maps with young children is limited to the discussion of the four Habits of Mind most closely related to our recommendations using TMaps: (1) empathic, (2) metacognitive, (3) questioning, and (4) multisensory. Hyerle's teaching and research, particularly with

older learners, revealed how some more dynamic and adaptive graphic organizers and brainstorm webs may also be especially helpful in promoting the other 8 Habits of Mind. For example, graphic organizers have great utility in organizing vast quantities of facts and information as learners increasingly encounter content-dense textbooks, beginning in the upper elementary grades. Unfortunately, many graphic organizers arrive as preset, static formats to "fill in the blanks" and are not very adaptable. Blackline masters may be useful as short-term scaffolds, but over time they become reduced to simple memorization tools. This is not to say that graphic organizers and brainstorm webs are not helpful, as they too can play a similarly important role during circle time and classroom meetings with young children (e.g., using brainstorm webs to help children identify and choose topics for exploration and investigation during cooperative group projects). In order to reduce the confusion of visual tools in a classroom, teachers simply translate different graphic organizers and brainstorming webs into the common visual language of TMaps by identifying the cognitive processes common to both.

Developmentally, young children's inhibitory control (and its contribution toward the development of self-regulation) is facilitated and supported during TMap activities. As young children develop self-regulation, they increase their ability to successfully participate to the fullest extent possible, with increased confidence, interest, and subsequent learning. As Piaget (1971) notes, children's "interest" is the fuel (motivation) that drives their learning. Hence, children's increased interest in using TMaps becomes the critical motivation to learn, and simultaneously taps into the other Habits of Mind behaviors, including perseverance, creativity, flexibility, and curiosity.

While supporting children in improving "learning" outcomes based on content objectives has been the traditional primary focus of education, learning how to consciously improve one's ability to "think" is steadily shifting the paradigm in the 21st century. This is especially true as children are now engaged in more virtual, independent learning, and as "content" can be accessed easily from the internet. Further, a learner's ability to filter, evaluate, reflect, and self-assess their own learning and thinking is becoming an essential dimension of the virtual-tech age.

Empathetic Understanding and Process Learning

Young children's ability to regulate their attention, behavior, and emotions helps to set the stage, and position them to understand and appreciate others' lived experiences, interpretations, and perspectives shared, discussed, debated, and negotiated during TMap activities. As observed by Hyerle (2000), empathetic understanding is a reciprocal process that requires more than a mere recapitulation of a peer's thoughts and emotions. Instead, an authentically empathetic understanding engages an even deeper sense of connection and interpretation between the learner's internal (mental) map and the visual map shared by a classmate within the multiple frames of reference influencing (and informing) the completed maps.

When young children use a Double-Bubble Map, such as to compare and contrast foods (science), countries (social studies), or books (language arts), differences in opinions, perspectives, interpretations, or lived experiences will likely emerge across different groups of children.

Differences in the information, concepts, and relationships that children select to convey using TMaps can vary, as seen in a map that compares carrots and oranges. For example, some children may have differing opinions as to whether carrots and oranges "taste good" or how they like to eat them, such as cooked or raw (Figure 6.4)

Children's perspectives are based largely on and influenced and informed by their individual identities (based in part on gender, culture, ethnicity, language, development, SES, community, and region) and related lived experiences. Recognizing and capitalizing on the culturally responsive benefits of TMaps are further discussed in Chapter 4, and likewise noted in relation to children choosing their favorite foods to write about using their five senses in Chapter 5. Therefore, children must rely on their self-regulation and empathetic understanding to consider, contemplate, appreciate, and value the divergent perspectives they encounter across their peers' individual TMaps. Further, children's individual perspectives are mindfully noted and

Figure 6.4. Double-Bubble Map: Comparing and Contrasting Carrots and Oranges

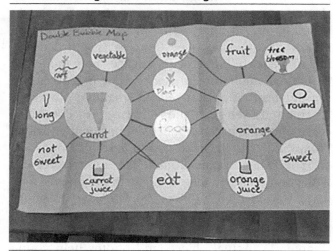

highlighted using the reflective Frame of Reference as well. Noted differences do not necessarily translate into opposing right/wrong or good/bad dichotomies but, rather, reveal a range of possible answers, viewpoints, and interpretations.

Learning about new and multiple perspectives and varied lived experiences shared by their peers within diverse, inclusive, democratic learning communities (as described in Chapter 4) serves to expand, enrich, and deepen children's schema of understanding better than through the limitations of their own situated realities. As children complete individual maps, they have the luxury to enact their own voice, identity, and agency (see Chapter 4) by independently choosing the concepts and information that matters most to them. Educational approaches that emphasize children's individual strengths and funds of knowledge, like TMaps, create interactive and inclusive learning environments where *all* children can thrive. Individual maps can then be compared and contrasted to not only reveal the similarities and differences they have with their classmates, but more importantly, to help peers fully value and appreciate them.

Metacognitive Process Learning

Metacognition, as explained in Chapter 2, refers to the complex process of drawing from various mental resources whenever learners confront an unexpected dilemma or obstacle; find it necessary to plan a course of action; systematically review that strategy while executing it; and then reflect on the strategy in order to evaluate its effectiveness in terms of the intended outcomes (Hyerle, 1996, 2009). Hyerle developed and refined the eight TMaps and Frame of Reference specifically to promote learners' metacognitive development, by helping them (regardless of age) "think about their thinking" (Hyerle & Alper, 2011, p. 57) as they learn how to make their thoughts "visual." In his definition of TMaps, Dr. Arthur Costa called this language for thinking a form of "displayed metacognition" (as cited by Hyerle & Alper, 2011, p. xviii).

This book strives to make young children's metacognitive experiences using TMaps even more tactile with the use of concrete maps and materials. When learners become fluent with TMaps and begin self-selecting the type of TMap(s) to use for a particular learning activity, they are in fact mindfully engaged in the process of metacognition. In effect, learners are now independently deciding and self-selecting whether sequencing, or classifying, or identifying causes and effects, or analogies are the most effective cognitive processes (and corresponding TMaps) required to best learn the content in front of them. Children are not waiting to be *told* how to think; rather, the TMaps empower them to become *reflective* thinkers and learners on their own right.

After multiple, ongoing experiences using TMaps in whole-group settings, children quickly begin to connect each TMap with its corresponding metacognitive process (e.g., Circle Map with brainstorming; Bubble Map with describing), as described and illustrated in each chapter of this book. Varying the different Thinking Map metacognitive applications according to children's individual strengths, development, interests, talents, aptitudes, culture, language, prior knowledge, and experiences is an important aspect of what early childhood educators consider to be developmentally appropriate practice. As a flexible, adaptable teaching and learning framework, TMaps help teachers and children achieve developmentally appropriate standards.

ALIGNMENT WITH STANDARDS

It is critical for educators to understand how teaching young children with Thinking Maps complement and support local, state, and national Pre-K–2

standards for learning and development. TMaps have a clear and definitive focus on cognitive, language, and socioemotional development, with direct application to the different academic content areas. In *Thinking Maps: A Language for Learning*, Hyerle and Yeager (2018) state that these content-based standards are directly correlated to the TMaps and are a central dimension of the professional learning and development process. Standards provide helpful learning and developmental benchmarks used to guide and inform learning goals and objectives. Subsequent instructional practices are carefully and strategically selected by educators to teach and achieve targeted standards.

The urgent need to select developmentally appropriate standards and practices to meet children's individual developmental and learning rates in ways that are culturally sensitive, responsive, and respectful across diverse groups of children cannot be overstated. It is equally imperative for teachers (and administrators) to understand that Thinking Maps have not been designed to somehow speed up or accelerate children's learning and development. Likewise, teachers should not use TMaps to "push" individual children's academic acquisition beyond their individual rates of learning and development. To do this would be a gross misuse (and arguably, abuse) of this learning–teaching framework that would result in developmentally "inappropriate" practice. Hence, the selection of developmentally appropriate standards aligned with using TMaps in developmentally appropriate ways is paramount.

Early Learning Standards and Guidelines

In recent decades, individual states within the United States have moved forward with initiatives to strengthen early childhood programming and emphasize greater accountability for child outcomes; these include the development of Early Learning Guidelines (Administration for Children & Families Office of Child Care, 2015). The Office of Child Care reports that significant progress has been made in developing and implementing Early Learning Guidelines (ELGs). All 56 states and territories have developed ELGs for preschool children.

The emphasis on "developmentally appropriate" standards and guidelines was also noted in the Race to the Top Early Learning Challenge (RTT-ELC) program application, using the term "Early Learning and Development Standards" as interchangeable with Early Learning Guidelines. Similar to the developmental domains discussed earlier, the U.S. Department of Education identifies five domains of school readiness: (1) language and literacy development, (2) cognition and general knowledge (including early mathematics and early scientific development), (3) approaches toward learning, (4) physical well-being and motor development, and (5) social and emotional development (National Education Goals Panel, 1995, p. 3). Irrespective of the framework adopted by states for the purpose of developing ELGs, the standards for Early Learning and Development should entail "a set of expectations, guidelines, or developmental milestones" that

- Describe what all children from birth to kindergarten entry should know and be able to do and their disposition toward learning
- Are appropriate for each age group (e.g., infants, toddlers, and preschoolers); for English learners; and for children with disabilities or developmental delays
- Cover all essential domains of school readiness
- Are universally designed and developmentally, culturally, and linguistically appropriate (Office of Child Care, 2016).

Throughout this book, TMap activities and materials are recommended that are age appropriate developmentally and culturally for diverse groups of young children (ages 3–8), including dual language learners and children with disabilities. Regardless of which state-level ELGs are employed, all teachers should readily find clear alignments with using TMaps to help satisfy and address ELGs across the domains. The metacognitive processes promoted by Thinking Maps further support executive function skills and self-regulation development that research identifies as critical school readiness skills.

At the national level, The Head Start Early Learning Outcomes Framework (Administration for Children & Families Office of Child Care, 2015) follows the five domains of school readiness identified by the U.S. Department of Education. The key executive function skills (working memory, cognitive flexibility, and inhibitory control) and self-regulation skills are central

components of the approaches to learning domain and actively promoted by Thinking Maps. Across the socioemotional, language and literacy, and cognitive domains, guideline components that align with, and are promoted by, TMap activities include

- Positive relationships and interactions with adults and other children
- Prosocial and cooperative behavior with adults and other children
- Use of problem-solving skills
- Understanding, implementing, and responding to increasingly complex communication and language
- Recognizing pictures, symbols, signs, or words
- Comprehending pictures and stories
- Understanding and using a variety of words for a variety of purposes
- Understanding word categories and relationships among words
- Understanding print and function of words
- Understanding narrative structure through storytelling/retelling
- Asking and answering questions about a book
- Exploring people and objects
- Understanding causal relationships
- Recognizing differences among familiar and unfamiliar people, objects, actions, or events
- Using memories as foundations for more complex actions and thoughts
- Using a variety of strategies in solving problems
- Matching and sorting objects or people to understand similar and different
- Using objects or symbols to represent something else
- Understanding simple patterns
- Comparing and categorizing observable phenomena
- Asking questions, gathering information, and making predictions
- Analyzing results, drawing conclusions, and communicating results

Many of the developmental skills promoted in the early years as "pre-academic" also appear in the kindergarten and primary grade academic standards.

Elementary Standards and Guidelines

Much like the early learning standards and guidelines above, teachers can readily see the alignments between Thinking Maps and the different state-level and national elementary content standards. In addition to a clear alignment with language and literacy standards, TMaps can likewise support mathematical thinking (as illustrated by the *Goldilocks and the Three Bears* example and others), science, and social studies. Widely used curriculum standards include the Next Generation Science Standards (NGSS Lead States, 2013), C3 Framework for Social Studies State Standards, and Common Core State Standards for English Language Arts and Math. Since the eight metacognitive processes promoted by Thinking Maps are used to learn, understand, and apply academic content knowledge and skills, teachers can easily cite content standards that are addressed using Thinking Map activities.

CONCLUSION

This book has outlined the many learning and developmental benefits for using Thinking Maps® with young children (ages 3–8). TMaps' eight corresponding metacognitive processes together with the Frame of Reference provide young children with important learning opportunities to develop the key executive function skills (cognitive flexibility, working memory, and inhibitory control) as well as self-regulation. EF and self-regulation development are deemed as essential school readiness skills needed to ensure successful transition to kindergarten, continued academic success, and later life outcomes. Relatedly, four of the Habits of Mind promoted by Thinking Maps further support children's active participation and long-term school success.

While Thinking Maps definitively guide and facilitate children's cognitive development, benefits across other domains and academic content areas have been thoroughly illustrated and discussed, with clear alignments to standards. It is imperative that TMap activities are implemented in developmentally and culturally responsive, sensitive, and respectful ways across diverse groups of children within inclusive, democratic settings, as illustrated throughout this book, and will therein reside in the hearts and minds of every learner and educator.

Glossary

Successful implementation requires educators over time, to fully grasp the concepts, constructs, and skills related to Thinking Maps. This list of terms provides a quick guide and reference as educators learn how to best implement Thinking Maps with the full range of young diverse learners to promote cognition, metacognition, and overall development across all domains and academic content areas.

Brain—Central nervous system organ is a "pattern detector" that makes sense of the world by constructing patterns from the world (Caine & Caine, 1994). The brain-mind detects and constructs patterns into schemas of understanding that are the essence of intelligence in action (Goleman, 1985, pp. 82–83). Mapping is what the brain does. The brain-mind naturally performs multidimensional mapping of mental models when processing and crafting information into knowledge (Hyerle, 2009, pp. 11–12).

Conceptual Mapping—Offers a rich synthesis of creative, analytical, and connective conceptual processes (Hyerle, 2009, p. 21).

Concreteness—Embodies knowledge in materials and equipment (Gage, 1974; McTighe & Lyman, 1988).

Frame of Reference—A metacognitive stance visually represented in the Thinking Maps model as a rectangle drawn by learners around each map.

Graphic Organizers—Blackline masters that are "pre-structured" for children to fill in words without changes on paper, arranged to represent an individual's understanding of the relationship between words that take form from the presumed structure of relationships among ideas (Clarke, 1991, p. 30). They further illustrate concepts and interrelationships among concepts in a text, using diagrams or other pictorial devices across content area (Hyerle, 2009, p. 25).

Knowledge—Defined as the basic organization of content (Bloom, 1956).

Mapping—A metaphor for connecting and overlapping tools for mental fluency. Forming a rich synthesis of thinking processes, mental strategies, techniques, and knowledge enables humans to investigate unknowns and show patterns of information that can then be used to express, build, and assess new knowledge and understanding (Hyerle, 2009, p. 14).

Maps—Adaptable visual displays used to relate new information to other information (Caine & Caine, 1994, p. 46).

Mental Model—Theory or framework that a person—or a group—construct for how a system or part of a system works (Hyerle, 2000, p. 95).

Metacognition—Mental resources drawn from when confronted with a dilemma or some obstacle to plan a course of action, monitor that strategy while executing it, then reflect on the strategy to evaluate its productiveness in terms of the outcomes it was intended to achieve (Hyerle, 1996, p. ix; 2009, pp. xi–xii). Popularized as "thinking about thinking" in the *Put Reading First* document (Armbruster et al., 2009).

Patterns of Thinking—Designs that expand, overlap, and layer information for making meaning (Hyerle, 1990, 1996, 2000).

Process—Highest form of learning and the most appropriate base for curriculum change. In education, it is a perpetual endeavor that employs knowledge not merely as a composite of information, but as a system for continuous learning (Hyerle, 2009, p. xiii).

Schemas—Intelligence in action, influenced by social-emotional background experiences, that guides the analysis of sensory input (Goleman, 1985, pp. 82–83).

Semantic Maps—Predominantly used to describe brainstorming webs for writing process and language arts instruction (Hyerle, 1996, p. 24).

Systems Thinking—The unique capacity to see the parts in relationship to the whole while recognizing the boundaries and the interactions between the interconnecting parts (Hyerle, 2009, pp. xii–xiii).

Thinking—May be understood (or conceived) as the capacity of the learner to read and understand patterns, whether embedded in text (Hyerle, 2000, p. 105) or observed and experienced within their surroundings (Piaget, 1971).

Thinking Maps—A model used as a language or integrated tool kit according to eight thinking-process maps, developed by Hyerle (1988–1993) that are graphically consistent and flexible so

that children can easily expand the map to reflect the content pattern studied and learned (Hyerle, 2009, p. 120).

Thinking Process Maps—Hands-on graphic, schematic mental models of concepts used to help children draw secondary abstract concepts that cannot be held in their hands (Hyerle, 2000, p. 84) due to cognitive load, complexity, and processes of assimilation and accommodation (Piaget, 1959).

Thinking Visual Tools—Forms of metacognition that are used to graphically display thinking processes—such as Thinking Maps (Hyerle, 1996, p. ix).

Visual Tools—Symbols graphically linked by mental associations to create a pattern of information and form knowledge about an idea (Clarke, 1991). As linguistic, visual, spatial, symbol systems, visual tools are used by learners, teachers, and leaders to graphically link mental and emotional associations, thus creating and communicating socially and collaboratively rich patterns of thinking while negotiating meaning and networking ideas (Hyerle, 2009, p.xix).

References

Administration for Children & Families Office of Child Care. (2015). Head Start early learning outcomes framework: Ages birth to five. Administration for Children & Families Office of Child Care.

Akiba, M., LeTendre, G. K., & Scribner, J. P. (2007). Teacher quality, opportunity gap, and national achievement in 46 countries. *Educational Researcher, 36*, 369–387.

Alvarez, A., & Booth, A. E. (2014). Motivated by meaning: Testing the effect of knowledge-infused rewards on preschoolers' task persistence. *Child Development, 123*, 783–791. https://doi.org/10.1111/cdev.12151

Anastasi, A., & Urbina, S. (1997). *Psychological testing* (7th ed.). Prentice Hall.

Armbruster, B. B., Lehr, F., Osborn, J., & Adler, C. R. (2009). *Put reading first: The research building blocks of reading instruction: Kindergarten thru grade 3* (3rd ed.). National Institute for Literacy.

Baillargeon, R., Wu, D., Yuan, S., Li, J., & Luo, Y. (2009). Young infants' expectations about self-propelled objects. In B. M. Hood and L. Santos (Eds.), *The origins of object knowledge*. Oxford University Press.

Ballou, D., Sanders, W. L., & Wright, P. (2004). Controlling for student background in value-added assessment of teachers. *Journal of Educational and Behavioral Statistics, 29*(1), 37–65.

Barkman, R. C. (2021). Why the human brain is so good at detecting patterns. *Psychology Today* at www.psychologytoday.com/us/blog/singular-perspective/202105/why-the-human-brain-is-so-good-

Bauer, J. R., & Booth, A. E. (2019). Exploring potential cognitive foundations of scientific literacy in preschoolers: Causal reasoning and executive function. *Early Childhood Research Quarterly, 46*, 275–284. https://doi.org/10.1016/j.ecresq.2018.09.007

Bauer, J. R., Booth, A. E., & McGroarty-Torres, K. (2016). Causally-rich group play: A powerful context for building preschoolers' vocabulary. *Frontiers in Psychology, 7*, Article 997.

Belsky, J., & van Ijzendoorn, M. H. (2015). What works for whom? Genetic moderation of intervention efficacy. *Development and Psychopathology, 27* (Special Issue 01), 1–6.

Bierman, K. L., Nix, R. L, Greenberg, M. T., Blair, C., & Domitrovich, C. E. (2008a). Executive functions and school readiness intervention: Impact, moderation, and mediation in the Head Start REDI program. *Development and Psychopathology, 20*(3), 821–843.

Bierman, K. L., Domitrovich, C. E., Nix, R. L., Gest, S. D., Welsh, J. A., Greenberg, M. T., Blair, C., Nelson, K. E., & Gill, S. (2008b). Promoting academic and social-emotional school readiness: The Head Start REDI program. *Child Development, 79*(6), 1802–1817.

Bitter, & Loney, (2015). *Deeper Learning: Improving Students Outcomes for College, Career, and Civic Life*. Policy Brief. Education Policy Center at American Institutes for Research.

Blömeke, S., Suhl, U., & Kaiser, G. (2011). Teacher education effectiveness: Quality and equity of future primary teachers' mathematics and mathematics pedagogical content knowledge. *Journal of Teacher Education, 62*(2), 154–171.

Bloom, B. S. (Ed.). (1956). *Taxonomy of educational objectives. Handbook I: Cognitive domains*. McKay.

Bodovski, K., & Farkas, G. (2007). Mathematics growth in early elementary school: The roles of beginning knowledge, student engagement, and instruction. *The Elementary School Journal, 108*(2), 115–130.

Bodrova, E., & Leong, D. (2007). *Tools of the mind: The Vygotskian approach to early childhood education* (2nd ed.). Pearson/Merrill Prentice Hall.

Bonawitz, E., Shafto, P., Gweon, H., Goodman, N. D., Spelke, E., & Schulz, L. E. (2011). The double-edged sword of pedagogy: Instruction limits spontaneous exploration and discovery. *Cognition, 120*(3), 322–330. https://doi.org/10.1016/j.cognition.2010.10.001

Booth, A. E. (2009). Causal supports for early word learning. *Child Development, 80*(4), 1243–1250.

Booth, A. E., Shavlik, M., & Haden, C. A. (2020). Parents' causal talk: Links to children's causal stance

and emerging scientific literacy. *Developmental Psychology, 56*(11), 2055–2064. https://doi.org/10.1037/dev0001108

Booth, A. E., Waxman, S. R., & Huang, Y. T. (2005). Conceptual information permeates word learning in infancy. *Developmental Psychology, 41*, 491–505.

Bor, D. (2012). *The Ravenous Brain*. Basic Books.

Bowers, E. P., & Vasilyeva, M. (2011). The relation between teacher input and lexical growth of preschoolers. *Applied Psycholinguistics, 32*(1): 221–241.

Boyce, W. T., & Kobor, M. S. (2015). Development and the epigenome: The "synapse" of gene-environment interplay. *Developmental Science, 18*(1), 1–23.

Boykin, A. W., Watkins, W., Lewis, J., & Chou, V. (2000). *The challenges of cultural socialization in the schooling of African American elementary school children: Exposing the hidden curriculum, race and education*. Allyn & Bacon.

Bredekamp, S. (2011). *Effective practices in early childhood education: Building a foundation*. Pearson.

Brenneman, K., Stevenson-Boyd, J., & Frede, E. C. (2009). *Math and science in preschool: Policies and practice*. National Institute for Early Education Research.

Brooks, J. G. (2011). *Big science for growing minds*. Teachers College Press.

Busch, J. T., Willard, A. K., & Legare, C. H. (2018). Explanation scaffolds causal learning and problem solving in childhood. In M. M. Saylor & P. A. Ganea (Eds.), *Active learning from infancy to childhood* (pp. 113–127). Springer. https://doi.org/10.1007/978-3-319-77182-3_7

Butler, L. P. (2020). The empirical child? A framework for investigating the development of scientific habits of mind. *Child Development Perspectives, 14*(1), 34–40. https://doi.org/10.1111/cdep.12354

Caine, R. N., & Caine, G. (1994). *Making connections: Teaching and the human brain*. Addison-Wesley Pub. Co.

Camera, L. (2017, August). New study questions link between race, disability in students. *U.S. News*. www.usnews.com/new/education-news/articles/2017-08-31/new-study-questions-links-between-race-disability-in-students

Cameron, C. E. (2018). *Hands on, minds on: How executive function, motor, and spatial skills foster school readiness*. Teachers College Press.

Carey, S. (2009). *The origin of concepts*. Oxford University Press.

Castro, D. C., Ayankoya, B., & Kasprzak, C. (2011). *The new voices, nuevas voces guide to cultural and linguistic diversity in early childhood*. Paul H. Brookes Publishing Co.

CDC (Centers for Disease Control and Prevention). (2014). *Middle childhood (6–8 years of age); Developmental milestones*. www.cdc.gov/ncbdd/childdevelopment/positiveparenting/iddle.html

Center for American Progress and the Council of Chief State School Officers. (2014). *Next-generation accountability systems: An overview of current state policies and practices*. Center for American Progress and the Council of Chief State School Officers.

Center on the Developing Child at Harvard University. (2016). *Applying the Science of Child Development in Child Welfare Systems*. www.developingchild.harvard.edu

Center on the Developing Child at Harvard University. (2021). *Three Principles to Improve Outcomes for Children and Families, 2021 Update*. www.developingchild.harvard.edu

Chappuis, J., Stiggins, R. J., Chappuis, S., & Arter, J. A. (2011). *Classroom assessment for student learning: Doing it right—Using it well*. 2nd edition. Pearson.

Chow, B. (2010). The quest for deeper learning. *Education Week*. Retrieved from www.hewlett.org/newsroom/news/quest-deeper-learning-barbara-chow

Civil, M. (2018). A commentary on identifying and connecting to family and community funds of knowledge. In T. G. Bartell (Ed.), *Toward Equity and Social Justice in Mathematics Education* (pp. 145–149). Springer.

Claessens, A., Engel, M., & Curran, F. C. (2014). Academic content, student learning, and the persistence of preschool effects. *American Educational Research Journal, 51*(2), 403–434.

Clarke, J. H. (1991). *Patterns of thinking*. Allyn and Bacon.

Clements, D. H., & Sarama, J. (2009). *Learning and teaching early math: The learning trajectories approach*. 1st edition. Routledge.

Clements, D. H., & Sarama, J. (2012). Learning and teaching early and elementary mathematics. In J. S. Carlson & J. R. Leving (Eds.), *Instructional strategies for improving students' learning: Focus on early reading and mathematics* (pp. 107–162). Information Age Publishing.

Clements, D. H., & Sarama, J. (2014). *Learning and teaching early math: The learning trajectories approach*. 2nd edition. Routledge.

Collaborative for Academic, Social, and Emotional Learning. (2015). www. https://casel.org/social-and-emotional-learning/core-competencies

Cooper, D. H., Roth, E. P., Speece, D. L., & Schatschnieder, C. (2002). The contribution of oral language skills to the development of phonological awareness. *Applied Psycholinguistics, 23*, 399–416.

Connor, C. M., Alberto, P. A., Compton, D. L., O'Connor, R. E., & National Center for Special Education Research. (2014). *Improving reading outcomes for students with or at risk for reading disabilities: A synthesis of the contributions from the Institute of Education Science Research Centers*. NCSER 2014–3000. National Center for Special Education Research.

Copley, J. V. (2007). *Mathematics: The creative curriculum approach*. Teaching Strategies.

Costa, A. L., ed. (1999). *Developing minds: A resource book for teaching thinking* (rev. ed., Vols. 1 and 2). Association for Supervision and Curriculum Development.

Costa, A. L., & Kallick, B. (2000). *Activating and engaging habits of mind*. Association for Supervision and Curriculum Development.

Counsell, S. (2007). *What Happens When Veteran and Beginner Teachers' Life Histories Intersect with High-stakes Testing and What Does It Mean for Learners and Teaching Practice: The Making of a Culture of Fear*. EdD diss., University of Northern Iowa.

Counsell, S. (2009). Abandoning the least restrictive environment in favor of natural settings: The achievement of social justice for all—It's a right not a privilege! *The Constructivist, 20*(1), 1–30, ISSN 1091–4072.

Counsell, S. L. (2011). Becoming "science experimentors"—Tenets of quality professional development and how they can reinvent early science learning experiences. *Science and Children, 49*(2), 52–56.

Counsell, S. (2017). Promoting STEM with the full range of learners: Using ramps and pathways. *Exchange, 39*(3), 80–82. www.childcareexchange.com/article/promoting-stem-*with-the-full-range-of-learners*/5023582/

Counsell, S. L., & Boody, R. M. (2013). Social pedagogy and liberal egalitarian compensatory programs: The case of Head Start. *Education Policy Analysis Archives, 21*(39). http://epaa.asu.edu/ojs/article/view/1299

Counsell, S., Escalada, L., Geiken, R., Sander, M., Uhlenberg, J., Van Meeteren, B., Yoshizawa, S., & Zan, B. (2016). *STEM learning with young children: Inquiry teaching with Ramps and Pathways*. Teachers College Press.

Counsell, S. L., & Geiken, R. (2019). Improving STEM teaching practices with R&P: Increasing the full range of children's STEM outcomes. *Journal of Early Childhood Teacher Education, 40*(4), 352–381. https://doi.org/10.1080/10901027.2019.1603173

Counsell, S., Jacobs, K., & Gatewood, S. (2017). What's in our soil? A university-nonprofit-school partnership aims to raise environmental awareness. *Science and Children, 55*(1), 58–64.

Counsell, S., Palmer, M., & Peat, F. (2020). Full STEAM ahead with shape, bake, and grow! Taking to the outdoors in urban settings encourages plant knowledge and healthy lifestyles. *Science & Children, 57*(9), 47–53. http://digital.nsta.org/publication/?i=664080&article_id=3698920&view=articleBrowser&ver=html5

Counsell, S., & Peat, F. (2017). Increasing STEM outcomes through quality collaborations: It takes a village to prepare high quality STEM educators. *Connected Science Learning, 1* (4): Part 2. Retrieved from http://csl.nsta.org/2017/11/increasing-stem-outcomes

Counsell, S., & Sander, M. (2016). Using ramps in diverse learning communities. In S. Counsell, L. Escalada, R. Geiken, M. Sander, J. Uhlenberg, B. Van Meeteren, & B. Zan, *STEM learning with young children: Inquiry teaching with Ramps and Pathways* (pp. 87–109). Teachers College Press.

Counsell, S., Uhlenberg, J., & Zan, B. (2013). Ramps and Pathways early physical science program: Preparing educators as science mentors. In R. Yager, S. Koba, and B. Wojnowski (Eds.), *Exemplary science: Best practices in professional development* (2nd ed., pp. 143–156). National Science Teachers Association Press.

Cunha, F., & Heckman, J. J. (2010). *Investing in our young people*. Working paper 1620. National Bureau of Economic Research.

Danko-McGhee, K., & Slutsky, R. (2011). Judging a book by its cover: Preschool children's aesthetic preferences for picture books. *International Journal of Education Through Art, 7*, 171–185. https://doi.org/10.1386/eta.7.2.171_1

Darling-Hammond, L. (2006). Securing the right to learn: Policy and practice for powerful teaching and learning. *Educational Researcher, 35*(7), 13–24.

Darling-Hammond, L., & Plank, D. N. (2015). *Supporting continuous improvement in California's education system*. Policy Analysis for California Education and Stanford Center for Opportunity Policy in Education.

Darling-Hammond, L., Wilhoit, G., & Pittenger, L. (2014). Accountability for college and career readiness: Developing a new paradigm. *Education Policy Analysis Archives, 22*(86), 1.

DEC. (2007). Promoting positive outcomes for children with disabilities: Recommendations for curriculum, assessment, and program evaluation. DEC.

De Deyne, S., & Storms, G. (2008). Word associations: Network and semantic properties. *Behavior Research Methods, 40*(1), 213–231.

DeLoache, J. S., Pickard, M. B., & LoBue, V. (2011). "How very young children think about animals" in *How animals affect us: Examining the influence of human-animal interaction on child development and human health*. In P. McCardle, S. McCune, J. A. Griffin, and V. Maholmes (Eds.), *American Psychological Association* (85–99). https://doi.org/10.1037/12301-004

Denham, S. A., & Brown, C. (2010). "Plays nice with others": Social-emotional learning and academic success. *Early Education and Development, 21*(5), 652–680.

Developmental Studies Center (DSC). (1996). Ways we want our class to be: Class meetings that build commitment to kindness and learning. DSC.

DeVries, R., & Sales, C. (2011). *Ramps & Pathways: A constructivist approach to physics with young children*. National Association for the Education of Young Children.

DeVries, R., & Zan, B. (2012). *Moral classrooms, moral children: Creating a constructivist atmosphere in early education*. 2nd edition. Teachers College Press.

DeVries, R., Zan, B., Hildebrandt, C., Edmiaston, R., & Sales, C. (2002). *Developing constructivist early childhood curriculum: Practical principles and activities*. Teachers College Press.

Diamond, A. (2013). Executive functions. *Annual Review of Psychology, 64*(1), 135–168. http://dx.doi.org/10.1146annurev-psych-113011-143750

Diamond, K. E., Justice, L. M., Siegler, R. S., & Snyder, P. A. (2013). *Synthesis of IES research on early intervention and early childhood education*. National Center for Special Education Research, Institute of Education Sciences, U.S. Department of Education.

Diamond, A., & Ling, D. S. (2016). Conclusions about interventions, programs, and approaches for improving executive functions that appear justified and those that despite much hype, do not. *Developmental Cognitive Neuroscience, 18*, 34–48.

Dickinson, D. K., & Porche, M. V. (2011). Relation between language experiences in preschool classrooms and children's kindergarten and fourth-grade language and reading abilities. *Child Development, 82*(3), 870–886.

Dodge, D. T., Rudick, S., & Berk, K. (2004). *The creative curriculum for infants, toddlers, and twos*. 2nd edition. Teaching Strategies.

Duke, N. K., & Block, M. K. (2012). Improving reading in the primary grades. *The Future of Children, 22*(2), 55–72.

Duncan, J. (2010). The multiple-demand (MD) system of the primate brain: Mental programs for intelligent behavior. *Trends in Cognitive Science, 14*, 172–179. https://doi.org/10.1016/j.tics.2010.01.004

Ehlert, L. (1995). *Snowballs*. Scholastic.

Elstgeest, J. (2001). The right question at the right time. In W. Harlen, *Primary science: Taking the plunge* (2nd ed.). Heinemann.

Engel, M., Claessens, A., & Finch, M. A. (2013). Teaching students what they already know? The (mis)alignment between mathematics instructional content and student knowledge in kindergarten. *Educational Evaluation and Policy Analysis, 35*(2), 157–178.

Epstein, A. S. (2007). *Essentials of active learning in preschool: Getting to know the High/Scope curriculum*. High/Scope Press.

Fagiolini, M., Jensen, C. L., & Champagne, F. A. (2009). Epigenetic influences on brain development and plasticity. *Current Opinion in Neurobiology, 19*(2), 207–212.

Farrant, B. M., & Zubrick, S. R. (2012). Early vocabulary development: The importance of joint attention and parent–child book reading. *First Language, 32*, 343–364. https://doi.org/10.1177/0142723711422626

Ford, D. Y., & Grantham, T. C. (2003). Providing access for culturally diverse gifted students: From deficit to dynamic thinking. *Theory into Practice, 42*, 217–225. https://doi.org/10.1207/x15430421tip4203_2

Fox, S. E., Levitt, P., & Nelson, C. A. (2010). How the timing and quality of early experiences influence the development of brain architecture. *Child Development, 81*(1), 28–40.

Gage, N. L. (1974). *Teacher effectiveness and teacher education: The search for a scientific basis*. Pacific Books.

Gallets, M. (2005). Storytelling and Story Reading: A Comparison of Effects and Children's Memory and Story Comprehension. MA Thesis, East Tennessee State University, Johnson City, Tennessee. http://dc.etsu.edu/cgi/viewcontent.cgi?article=2180&context=etd

Gámez, P. B., & Levine, S. C. (2013). Oral language skills of Spanish-speaking English language learners: The impact of high-quality native language exposure. *Applied Psycholinguistics, 34*(4): 673–696.

Gamire, E., & Pearson, G. (Eds.). (2006). Tech tally: Approaches to assessing technological literacy. National Academies Press.

Gelman, S. A. (2003). *The essential child: Origins of essentialism in everyday thought*. Oxford University Press.

Gerde, H. K., Schachter, R. E., & Wasik, B. A. (2013). Using the scientific method to guide learning: An integrated approach to early childhood curriculum. *Early Childhood Education Journal, 41*, 315–323.

Goleman, D. (1985). *Vital lies, simple truths: The psychology of self-deception*. Touchstone.

Gomi, T., & Stinchecum, A. M. (1993). *Everyone poops*. Kane/Miller.

Gonzales, P., Williams, T., Jocelyn, L., Roey, D., Kastberg, D., & Brenwald, S. (2008). *Highlights from TIMSS 2007: Mathematics and science achievement of U.S. fourth- and eighth-grade students in an international context (NCES 2009-001 revised)*. U.S. Department of Education, National Center for Education Statistics, Institute of Education Sciences.

Gopnik, A., & Nazzi, T. (2003). Words, kinds, and causal powers: A theory perspective on early naming and categorization. In D. H. O. Rakison & M. Lisa (Eds.), *Early category and concept development* (pp. 303–329). Oxford University Press.

Gopnik, A., & Schulz, L. (Eds.). (2007). *Causal learning*. Oxford University Press.

Gopnik, A., & Wellman, H. M. (2012). Reconstructing constructivism: Causal models, Bayesian learning mechanisms, and the theory. *Psychological Bulletin, 138*(6), 1085–1108.

Gray, S., Green, S., Alt, M., Hogan, T., Kuo, T., Brinkley, S., et al. (2017). The structure of working memory in young children and its relation to intelligence. *Journal of Memory and Language, 92*, 183–201.

Greenfield, D. B., Jirout, J., Dominguez, X., Greenberg, A., Maier, M., & Fuccillo, J. (2009). Science in the preschool classroom: A programmatic research agenda to improve science readiness. *Early Education and Development, 20*(2), 238–264.

Greenwood, C., Buzhardt, J., Walker, D., Howard, W., & Anderson, R. (2011). Program-level influences on the measurement of early communication for infants and toddlers in early Head Start. *Journal of Early Intervention, 33*(2): 110–134.

Greif, M. L., Kemler Nelson, D. G., Keil, F. C., & Gutierrez, F. (2006). What do children want to know about animals and artifacts? Domain-specific requests for information. *Psychological Science, 17*, 455–459.

Griebling, S. (2011). Discoveries from a Reggio-inspired classroom: Meeting developmental deeds through the visual arts. *Art Education, 64*(2), 6–11.

Griffiths, T. L., Steyvers, M., & Tenenbaum, J. B. (2007). Topics in semantic representation. *Psychological Review, 114*(2), 211.

Grissmer, D. K., Grimm, J., Aiyer, S. M., Murrah, W. M., & Steele, J. S. (2010a). Fine motor skills and early comprehension of the world: Two new school readiness indicators. *Developmental Psychology, 46*(5), 1008–1017.

Grissmer, D. K., Grimm, J., Aiyer, S. M., Murrah, W. M., & Steele, J. S. (2010b). *New school readiness indicators*. Research brief. University of Virginia, Center for Advanced Study of Teaching and Learning.

Grissom, J. A., & Redding, C. (2016). Discretion and disproportionality: Explaining the underrepresentation of high-achieving students of color in gifted programs. *AERA Open, 2*(1), 1–25.

Guarino, C., Dieterle, S. G., Bargagliotti, A. E., & Mason, W. M. (2013). What can we learn about effective early mathematics reading? A framework for estimating causal effects using longitudinal survey data. *Journal of Research on Educational Effectiveness, 6*(2), 164–198.

Hamre, B. K. (2014). Teachers' daily interactions with children: An essential ingredient in effective early childhood programs. *Child Development Perspectives, 8*(4), 223–230.

Harris, P. L. (2012). *Trusting what you're told: How children learn from others*. Belknap Press of Harvard University.

Healy, S. D., & Hurly, T. A. (2004). Spatial learning and memory in birds. *Brain, Behavior, and Evolution, 63*, 211–220. https://doi.org/10.1159/000076782

Heckman, J. J. (2007). The economics, technology, and neuroscience of human capability formation. *Proceedings of the National Academy of Sciences of the United States of America, 104*(33), 13250–13255.

Heckman, J. J., Pinto, R., & Savelyev, P. (2013). Understanding the mechanisms through which an influential early childhood program boosted adult outcomes. *American Economic Review, 103*(6), 2052–2086.

Helm, J. H., & Katz, L. G. (2011). *Young investigators: The project approach in the early years*. 2nd edition. Teachers College Press.

Helm, J. H., & Snider, K. A. (Eds.). (2020). *Growing child intellect: The manifesto for engaged learning in the early years*. Teachers College Press.

Henrichs, L. F., Leseman, P. P. M., Broekhof, K., & Cohen de Lara, H. (2011). Kindergarten talk about science and Technology. In M. J. de Vries, H. van Keulen, S. Peters, and J. W. van der Molen (Eds.), *Professional development for primary teachers in science and technology: The Dutch VTB-Pro Project in an international perspective* (pp. 217–227). Sense Publishers.

Heroman, C., & Jones, C. (2004). *Literacy: The creative curriculum approach*. Teaching Strategies.

Hiebert, J. C. (1999). Relationships between research and the NCTM standards. *Journal for Research in Mathematics Education, 30*(1), 3–19.

Hiebert, J. C., & Grouws, D. A. (2007). The effects of classroom mathematics teaching on students' learning (pp. 371–404). In F.K.J. Lester (Ed.), *Second handbook of research on mathematics teaching and learning*, Vol. 1 (pp. 371–404). Information Age Publishing.

Holland, A. C., & Kensinger, E. A. (2010). Emotion and autobiographical memory. *Physics of Life Reviews, 7*, 88–131. https://doi.org/10.1016/j.plrev.2010.01.006

Hyerle, D. (1988–1993). *Expand your thinking* (Series: Pre-K-Grade 8). Innovative Sciences, Inc.

Hyerle, D. (1990). *Designs for thinking connectively*. Designs for Thinking.

Hyerle, D. (1993). *Thinking Maps as tools for multiple modes of understanding*. Unpublished doctoral dissertation, University of California, Berkeley, California.

Hyerle, D. (1995). *Thinking Maps: Tools for learning training manual*. Innovative Science, Inc.

Hyerle, D. (1996). *Visual tools for constructing knowledge*. Association for Supervision and Curriculum Development.

Hyerle, D. (2000). *A field guide to using visual tools*. Association for Supervision and Curriculum Development.

Hyerle, D. (Ed.). (2004). *Student successes with Thinking Maps®: School-based research, results, and models for achievement using visual tools*. Corwin.

Hyerle, D. (2009). *Visual tools for transforming information into knowledge*. Corwin Press.

Hyerle, D., & Alper, L. (Eds.). (2011). *Student successes with Thinking Maps.®* 2nd edition. Corwin.

Hyerle, D., Curtis, S., & Alper, L. (Eds.). (2004). *Student successes with Teaching Maps: School-based research, results and models for achievement using visual tools*. Corwin Press.

Hyerle, D., & Williams, K. M. (2011). Bifocal assessment in the cognitive age: Thinking Maps for assessing content learning and cognitive processes. In D. Hyerle & L. Alper (Eds.), *Student successes with Thinking Maps®* (pp. 204–216). Corwin.

Hyerle, D., & Yeager, C. (2018). *Thinking Maps: A language for learning*. Thinking Maps, Inc.

Institute of Medicine (IOM). (2015). *Cognitive aging: Progress in understanding and opportunities for action*. The National Academies Press.

Institute of Medicine (IOM) & National Research Council (NRC). (2015). *Transforming the workforce for children birth through age 8: A unifying foundation*. The National Academies Press.

Isaacs, J. B. (2012). *Starting school at a disadvantage: The school readiness of poor children*. The Brookings Institution.

Jackson, Y. (2011). Closing the "gap" by connecting culture, language, and cognition. In D. N. Hyerle & L. Alper (Eds.), *Student successes with Thinking Maps.®* 2nd edition (pp. 51–60). Corwin Press.

Jacoby, J. W., & Lesaux, N. K. (2014). Support for extended discourse in teacher talk with linguistically diverse preschoolers. *Early Education and Development, 25*(8): 1162–1179.

Jalongo, M. R., & Isenberg, J. P. (2012). *Exploring your role in early childhood education*. 4th edition. Merrill.

Jirout, J., & Zimmerman, C. (2015). Development of science process skills in the early childhood years. In K. C. Trundle and M. Sackes (Eds.), *Research in early childhood science education* (pp. 143–165). Springer. https://doi.org/10.1007.978-94-017-9505-0_7

Kamii, C., & DeVries, R. (1978/1993). *Physical knowledge in preschool education: Implications of Piaget's theory*. Teachers College Press.

Keats, E. J. (1962). *The snowy day*. Viking Press.

Kelemen, D., Widdowson, D., Posner, T., Brown, A. L., & Casler, K. (2003). Teleo-functional constraints on preschool children's reasoning about living things. *Developmental Science, 6*, 329–345.

Kelly, K., & Phillips, S. (2016). *Teaching literacy to learners with dyslexia: A multi-sensory approach*. Sage Publications.

Kermani, H., & Aldemir, J. (2015). Preparing children for success: integrating science, math, and technology in early childhood classrooms. *Early Child Development and Care, 185*(9), 1504–1527.

Kim, H., Duran, C. A., Cameron, C. E., & Grissmer, D. W. (2018). Developmental relations among motor and cognitive processes and mathematics skills. *Child Development, 89*(2), 476–494. https://doi.org/10.1111/cdev.12752.

Kipping, P., Gard, A., Gilman, L., & Gorman, J. (2012). *Speech and Language development chart*. 3rd edition. Pro-Ed.

Klahr, D., & Chen, Z. (2003). Overcoming the positive-capture strategy in young children: Learning about indeterminacy. *Child Development, 74*(5), 1275–1296.

Kliewer, C. (1998). The meaning of inclusion. *Mental Retardation, 36*(4), 317–322.

Koenig, M. A., & Doebel, S. (2013). Children's understanding of unreliability: Evidence for a negativity bias. In M. R. Banaji and S. A. Gelman (Eds.), *Navigating the social world* (pp. 235–240). Future Horizons, Inc.

Kohn, A. (1999). *The schools our children deserve: Moving beyond traditional classrooms and tougher standards*. Houghton Mifflin.

Kohn, A. (2005). The trouble with pure freedom: A case for active adult involvement in progressive education. Alternative Education Resource Organization [AERO] Conference, Keynote Address, Washington, DC.

Kohn, A. (2006). *Beyond discipline: From compliance to community*. 2nd edition. Association for Supervision and Curriculum Development.

Kotaman, H., & Tekin, A. K. (2017). Informational and fictional books: Young children's book preferences and teachers' perspectives. *Early Child Development and Care, 187*, 600–614. https://doi.org/10.1080/03004430.2016.1236092

Kuhn, D. (2011). What is scientific thinking and how does it develop? In U. Goswami (Ed.), *The Wiley-Blackwell handbook of childhood cognitive development* (pp. 497–523). Wiley-Blackwell.

Kurzweil, R. (2012). *How to create a mind—The secret of human thought revealed*. Penguin Books.

Lam, L. L., Emberly, E, Fraser, H. B., Neumann, S. M., Chen, E., Miller, G. E., & Kobor, M. S. (2012). Factors underlying variable DNA methylation in a human community cohort. *Proceedings of the National Academy of Sciences of the United States of America, 109* (Suppl. 2), 17253–17260.

Lavin, T. A., & Hall, D. G. (2001). Domain effects in lexical development: Learning words for foods and toys. *Cognitive Development, 16*, 929–950.

Lee, J. S. (2011). Size matters: Early vocabulary as a predictor of language and literacy competence. *Applied Psycholinguistics, 32*(1), 69–92.

Legare, C. H., & Lombrozo, T. (2014). Selective effects of explanation on learning during early childhood. *Journal of Experimental Child Psychology, 126*(0), 198–212. https://doi.org/10.1016/j.jecp.2014.03.001

Legare, C. H., Schult, C. A., Impola, M., & Souza, A. L. (2016). Young children revise explanations in response to new evidence. *Cognitive Development, 39*, 45–56. https://doi.org/10.1016/j.cogdev.2016.03.003

Leong, T. L., & Park, Y. S. (2016). Introduction. In T. L. Leong & Y. S. Park (Eds.), *Testing and assessment with persons & communities of color* (pp. 1–2). American Psychological Association.

Lesaux, N. K., & Kieffer, M. J. (2010). Exploring sources of reading comprehension difficulties among language minority learners and their classmates in early adolescence. *American Educational Research Journal, 47*(3), 596–632.

Levin, J. R. (1988). Elaboration-based learning strategies: Powerful theory = powerful application. *Contemporary Educational Psychology, 13*, 191–205.

Lewin-Benham, A. (2011). *Twelve best practices of early childhood education: Integrating Reggio and other inspired approaches.* Teachers College Press.

Lindsay, G. W. (2020). Convolutional neural networks as a model of the visual system: Past, present, and future. *Journal of Cognitive Neuroscience, 33*(10), 2017–2031.

Llopart, M., & Esteban-Guitart, M. (2018). Funds of knowledge in 21st century societies: Inclusive education practices for under-represented students: A literature review. *Journal of Curriculum Studies, 50*(2), 145–161.

London, J. (1994). *Froggy gets dressed.* Puffin Books.

Marcis, D. M., & Sobel, D. M. (2017). The role of evidence, diversity and explanation in 4- and 5-year-olds' resolution of counterevidence. *Journal of Cognition and Development, 18*(6), 358–374. https://doi.org/10.1080/15248372.2017.1323755

Marriott, S. (2002). Red in tooth and claw? Images of nature in modern picture books. *Children's Literature in Education, 33*, 175–183. https://doi.org/10.1023/A:1019677931406

Martens, M. L. (1999). Productive questions: Tools for supporting constructivist learning. *Science and Children, 36*(8), 24–27, 53–56.

Martin, B. (1996). *Brown bear, brown bear, what do you see?* Henry Holt and Company.

Marzano, R. J., Pickering, D. J., & Pollock, J. E. (2001). *Classroom instruction that works: Research-based strategies for increasing student achievement.* Association for Supervision and Curriculum Development.

Mashburn, A. J., Justice, M., Downer, T., & Pianta, R. C. (2009). Peer effects on children's language achievement during pre-kindergarten. *Child Development, 80*(3), 686–702.

Mattson, M. P. (2014). Superior pattern processing is the essence of the evolved human brain. *Frontiers in Neuroscience, 8* (Article 265), 1–17. https://doi.org/10.3389/fnins.2014.00265

McClelland, M. M., Cameron Ponitz, C. E., Messersmith, E. E., & Tominey, S. L. (2010). Self-regulation: The integration of cognition and emotion. In R. M. Lerner & W. E. Overton (Eds.), *The handbook of life-span development, Vol. 1: Cognition, biology, and methods* (pp. 509–553). Wiley & Sons.

McTighe, J., & Lyman Jr., F. T. (1988). Cueing for thinking in the classroom: The promise of theory-embedded tools. *Educational Leadership, 45*(7), 18–24.

McWilliams, M. S. (2017). *Beyond the flannel board: Story retelling strategies across the curriculum.* Redleaf Press.

Meaney, M. J. (2010). Epigenetics and the biological definition of gene x environment interactions. *Child Development, 81*(1), 41–79.

Meltzer, L. (Ed.). (2018). *Executive function in education: From theory to practice.* 2nd edition. Guilford Press.

Mills, C. M., Sands, K. R., Rowles, S. P., & Campbell, I. L. (2019). "I want to know more!": Children are sensitive to explanation quality when exploring new information. *Cognitive Science, 43*(1). e12706. https://doi.org/10.1111/cogs.12706

Moran, S., & Gardner, H. (2018). Hill, skill, and will: Executive function from a multiple-intelligences perspective. In L. Meltzer (Ed.), *Executive function in education: From theory to practice* (pp. 25–56). Guilford Press.

Nagy, W., & Townsend, D. (2012). Words are tools: Learning academic vocabulary as language acquisition. *Reading Research Quarterly, 47*(1), 91–108.

National Association for the Education of Young Children (NAEYC). (2012). 2010 NAEYC standards for initial and advanced early childhood professional preparation programs. NAEYC.

National Research Council [NRC] (2013). *Next Generation Science Standards: For states, by states.* The National Academies Press. https://doi.org/10.17226/18290

NICHD (National Institute of Child Health and Human Development) Early Child Care Research Network. (2005). A large-scale study of classroom quality and teacher and student behavior. *Elementary School Journal, 105*(3), 305–323.

National Mathematics Advisory Panel. (2008). *Foundations for success: The final report of the National Mathematics Advisory Panel.* U.S. Department of Education, Office of Planning, Evaluation and Policy Development.

National Research Council (NRC). (2009). *Mathematics in early childhood: Paths toward excellence and equity,* edited by C. T. Cross, T. A. Woods, and H. Schweingruber. The National Academies Press.

National Research Council (NRC). (2010). *Exploring the Intersection of Science Education and 21st Century Skills.* The National Academies Press.

National Science Teachers Association Press. https://doi.org/10.2505/9781938946042

Nayfield, L., Brenneman, K., & Gelman, R. (2011). Science in the classroom: Finding a balance between autonomous exploration and teacher-led instruction in preschool settings. *Early Education and Development,*

22(6), 970–988. http://dx.doi.org/1080/10409289.2010.507496

NEGP (National Education Goals Panel). (1995). Reconsidering children's early development and learning: Toward common views and vocabulary. NEGP.

NGSS Lead States. (2013). *Next generation science standards: For states by states*. National Academies Press.

Nichols, S., Glass, G., & Berliner, D. (2006). High-stakes testing and student achievement: Does accountability pressure increase student learning? *Education Policy Analysis Archives, 14*, (January). http://epaa.asu.edu/epaa/v14n1

Nichols, S., Glass, G., & Berliner, D. (2012). High-stakes testing and student achievement: Updated analyses with NAEP data. *Education Policy Analysis Archive, 20* (July). http://epaa.asu.edu/ojs/article/view/1048

Numeroff, L. J. (1985). *If you give a mouse a cookie*. HarperCollins.

O'Connor, R. E., Bocian, K., Beebe-Frankenberger, M., & Linklater, D. L. (2010). Responsiveness of students with language difficulties to early intervention in reading. *Journal of Special Education, 43*(4), 220–235.

O'Connor, R. E., Bocian, K. M., Sanchez, V., Beach, K. D., & Flynn, L. J. (2013). Special education in a four-year response to intervention (RTI) environment: Characteristics of students with learning disability and grade of identification. *Learning Disabilities Research and Practice, 26*, 98–112.

O'Connor, R. E., Bocian, K. M., Sanchez, V., & Beach, K. D. (2014). Access to a responsiveness to intervention model: Does beginning intervention in kindergarten matter? *Journal of Learning Disabilities, 47*(4), 307–328.

Office of Special Education and Rehabilitative Services. (2018). *4th Annual Report to Congress on the Implementation of the Individuals with Disabilities Education Act*. U.S. Department of Education. www.2.ed.gov/about/reports/annual/osep/2018/parts-b-c/40th-arc-for-idea.pdf

Olmedo, E. L. (1981). Testing linguistic minorities. *American Psychologist, 36*, 1078–1085.

Pagani, L., & Messier, S. (2012). Links between motor skills and indicators of school readiness at kindergarten entry in urban disadvantaged children. *Journal of Educational and Developmental Psychology, 2*(1), 95–107.

Perkins, S. C., Finegood, E. D., & Swain, J. E. (2013). Poverty and language development: Roles of parenting and stress. *Innovations in Clinical Neuroscience, 10*(4), 10. Retrieved from http://ncbi.nlm.nih.gov/pmc

Peterson, S. M., & French, L. (2008). Supporting young children's explanations through inquiry science in preschool. *Early Childhood Research Quarterly, 23*, 395–408.

Piaget, J. (1932/1965). *The moral judgment of the child*. Free Press.

Piaget, J. (1952). *The origins of intelligence in children* (M. Cook, Trans.). International Universities Press.

Piaget, J. (1959). *The language and thought of the child*. Routledge & Kegan Paul.

Piaget, J. (1971). *Biology and knowledge: An essay on the relations between organic regulations and cognitive processes*. University of Chicago Press.

Piaget, J. (1978). *Success and understanding*. Harvard University Press. (Original work published 1974)

Piaget, J. (1981). *Intelligence and affectivity*. Annual Reviews, Inc.

Pianta, R. C., & Stuhlman, M. W. (2004). Teacher–child relationships and children's success in the first years of school. *School Psychology Review, 33*(3), 444–458.

Proctor, S. L., Graves, S. L., & Esch, R. C. (2012). Assessing African American students for specific learning disabilities: The promises and perils of response to intervention. *Journal of Negro Education, 81*, 268–282.

Raudenbush, S. W. (2009). The Brown legacy and the O'Connor challenge: Transforming schools in the images of children's potential. *Educational Researcher, 38*(3), 169–180.

Raver, C. C., & Blair, C. (2016). Neuroscientific insights: Attention, working memory, and inhibitory control. *The Future of Children, 26*(2), 95–118.

Reardon, S. F. (2011). The widening academic achievement gap between the rich and the poor: New evidence and possible explanations. In R. Murnane & G. Duncan (Eds.), *Whither opportunity? Rising inequality in schools and children's life changes* (pp. 91–116). Russell Sage Foundation Press.

Reardon, S. F., Robinson-Cimpian, J. Pl, & Weathers, E. S. (2015). Patterns and trends in racial/ethnic and socioeconomic academic achievement gaps. In H. F. Ladd & M. E. Goertz (Eds.), *Handbook of research in education finance and policy*, 2nd edition (pp. 491–509). Routledge.

Reese, W. J. (2013). *Testing wars in the public schools: A forgotten history*. Harvard University Press.

Reynolds, C. R. (1982). Methods for detecting construct and predictive bias. In R. A. Berk (Ed.), *Handbook of methods for detecting bias* (pp. 192–227). Johns Hopkins University Press.

Rhodes, S. M., Booth, J. N., Palmer, L. E., Blythe, R. A., Delibegovic, M., & Wheate, N. J. (2016). Executive functions predict conceptual learning of science. *British Journal of Developmental Psychology, 34*, 261–275. http://dx.doi.org/10.111/bjdp.12129

Robertson, S.-J. L., & Reese, E. (2017). The very hungry caterpillar turned into a butterfly: Children's and parents' enjoyment of different book genres. *Journal of Early Childhood Literacy, 17*, 3–25. https://doi.org/10.1177/1468798415598354

Roopnarine, J., & Johnson, J. E. (2008). *Approaches to early childhood education* (5th ed.). Pearson.

Rose, D. H., & Meyer, A. (2002). *Teaching every student in the Digital Age: Universal design for learning*. Association for Supervision and Curriculum Development.

Rudd, L. C., Lambert, M. C., Satterwhite, M., & Zaier, A. (2008). Mathematical language in early childhood settings: What really counts? *Early Childhood Education Journal, 36*, 167–188.

Rueda, M. R., Checa, P., & Combita, L. M. (2012). Enhanced efficiency of the executive attention network after training in preschool children: Immediate changes and effects after two months. *Developmental Cognitive Neuroscience, 2*, S192–S204.

Russell, M. K., & Airasian, P. W. (2011). *Classroom assessment: Concepts and applications*. 7th edition. McGraw-Hill.

Rutter, M. (2006). *Genes and behavior: Nature–nurture interplay explained*. Blackwell.

Rutter, M. (2012). Achievements and challenges in the biology of environmental effects. *Proceedings of the National Academy of Sciences of the United States of America 109* (Suppl.2), 17149–17153.

Sackes, M., Trundle, K. C., Bell, R. L., & O'Connell, A. A. (2011). The influence of early science experience in kindergarten on children's immediate and later science achievement: Evidence from the early childhood longitudinal study. *Journal of Research in Science Teaching, 48*(2), 217–235.

Sackes, M., Trundle, K. C., & Bell, R. L. (2013). Science learning experiences in kindergarten and children's growth in science performance in elementary grades. *Education and Science, 38*(167), 114–127.

Samarapungavan, A., Patrick, H., & Mantzicopoulos, P. (2011). What kindergarten students learn in inquiry-based science classrooms. *Cognition and Instruction, 29*(4), 416–470.

Sarama, J., & Clements, D. H. (2009). *Early childhood mathematics education research: Learning trajectories for young children*. Routledge.

Sarama, J., Lange, A. A., Clements, D. H., & Wolfe, C. B. (2012). The impacts of an early mathematics curriculum on Oral language and literacy. *Early Childhood Research Quarterly, 27*(3), 489–502.

Saxe, R. (2013). The new puzzle of theory of mind development. In M. R. Baniji and S. A. Gelman (Eds.), *Navigating the social world: What infants, children, and other species can teach us*. Oxford University Press.

Schunn, C. (2009). How kids learn engineering: The cognitive science perspective. *The Bridge: Linking Engineering and Society, 39*(3), 32–37.

Schwarz, C. V., Passmore, C., & Reiser, B. J. (2017). Moving beyond "knowing about" science to making sense of the world. In C. V. Schwarz, C. Passmore, & B. J. Reiser (Eds.), *Helping students make sense of the world using next generation science and engineering practices* (pp. 3–21). NSTA.

Schweinhart, L. J., Montie, J., Xiang, Z., Barnett, W. S., Belfield, C. R., & Nores, M. (2005). *Lifetime effects: The High/Scope Perry Preschool study through age 40* (Monographs of the High/Scope Educational Research Foundation, 14). High/Scope Press.

Selden, S. (2000). Eugenics and the social construction of merit, race and disability. *Journal of Curriculum Studies, 32*(2), 235–252.

Sénéchal, M. (2010). "Reading books to young children: What it does and does not do." In D. Aram and O. Korat (Eds.), *Literacy development and enhancement across orthographies and cultures*, Vol. 2 (111–122). Springer. https://doi.org/10.1007/978-1-4419-0834-6_8

Shavlik, M., Bauer, J. R., & Booth, A. E. (2020). Children's preference for causal information in storybooks. *Frontiers in Psychology, 11.* https://doi.org/10.3389/fpsyg.2020.00666

Shavlik, M., Davis-Kean, P. E., Schwab, J. F., & Booth, A. E. (2020). Early word-learning skills: A missing link in understanding the vocabulary gap? *Developmental Science.* 2020;00:e13034. https://doi.org/10.1111/desc.13034

Shavlik, M., Köksal, O., French, B. F., Haden, C. A., Legare, C. H., & Booth, A. E. (2022). Contributions of causal reasoning to early scientific literacy. *Journal of Experimental Child Psychology, 224.* https://doi.org/10.1016/j.jecp.2022.105509

Shonkoff, J. P., & Garner, A. S. (2012). The lifelong effects of early childhood adversity and toxic stress. *Journal of the American Academy of Pediatrics, 129*(1), 232–246.

Siegel, D. J. (2001). *The developing mind: How relationships and the brain interact to shape who we are*. Guilford Press.

Singham, M. (1995). Race and intelligence: What are the issues? *Phi Delta Kappan, 77*, 271–278.

Smith, L. B., Colunga, E., & Yoshida, H. (2010). Knowledge as process: Contextually cued attention and early word learning. *Cognitive Science, 34*(7), 1287–1314. https://doi.org/10.1111/j.1551-6709.2010.01130.x

Smith, L. B., Jones, S. S., Landau, B., Gershkoff-Stowe, L., & Samuelson, L. (2002). Object name learning provides on-the-job training for attention. *Psychological Science, 13*(1), 13–19. https://doi.org/10.1111/1467-9280.00403

Stipek, D. (2004). Teaching practices in kindergarten and first grade: Different strokes for different folks. *Early Childhood Research Quarterly, 19*(4), 548–568.

Stipek, D., & Valentino, R. A. (2015). Early childhood memory and attention as predictors of academic growth trajectories. *Journal of Educational Psychology, 107*, 771–788. http://dx.doi.org/10.1037/edu0000004

Styles, D. (2001). *Class meetings: Building leadership, problem-solving and decision-making skills in the respectful classroom.* Pembroke Publishers.

Suggate, S., Schaughency, E., McAnally, H., & Reese, E. (2018). From infancy to adolescence: The longitudinal links between vocabulary, early literacy skills, oral narrative, and reading comprehension. *Cognitive Development, 47,* 82–95. https://doi.org/10.1016/j.cogdev.2018.04.005

Swanson, H. L. (2011). Working memory, attention, and mathematical problem solving: A longitudinal study of elementary school children. *Journal of Educational Psychology, 103,* 821–837. http://dx.doi.org/10.1037/a0025114

Takesian, A. E., & Hensch, T. K. (2013). Balancing plasticity/stability across brain development. *Progress in Brain Research, 207,* 3–34.

Tao, Y., Oliver, M., & Venville, G. (2012). Long-term outcomes of early childhood science education: Insights from a cross-national comparative case study on conceptual understanding of science. *International Journal of Science and Mathematics Education, 10*(6), 1269–1302.

Thelen, E. (2005). Dynamic systems theory and the complexity of change. *Psychoanalytic Dialogues, 15*(2), 255–283.

Thompson, R. A. (2006). Conversation and developing understanding: Introduction to the special issue. *Merrill-Palmer Quarterly, 52*(1), 1–16. https://doi.org/10.1353/mpq.2006.0008

Thompson, R. A. (2013). Attachment theory and research: Precis and prospect. In P. Zelazo (Ed.), *Oxford handbook of developmental psychology,* Vol. 2, (pp. 191–216). Oxford University Press.

Trafton, A. (2014). In the blink of an eye: MIT neuroscientists find the brain images seen for as little as 13 milliseconds. *MIT News* at https://news.mit.edu/2014/in-the-blink-of-an-eye-0116

Trilling, B. (2010). Defining competence in deeper learning. Draft report to the William and Flora Hewlett Foundation. Hewlett Foundation.

Uncapher, M. R., & Rugg, M. D. (2005). Effects of divided attention on fMRI correlates of memory encoding. *Journal of Cognitive Neuroscience, 17,* 1923–1935.

Upton, A. (1960). *Design for thinking.* Pacific Books.

U.S. Department of Health & Human Services, Administration for Children and Families, Administration on Children, Youth and Families, Children's Bureau. (2016). *Child maltreatment 2014.* ii. www.acf.hhs.gov/programs/cb/research-data-technology/statistics-research/child-maltreatment

van den Heuvel-Panhuizen, M., & Elia, I. (2012). Developing a framework for the evaluation of picture books that support kindergartners' learning of mathematics. *Research in Mathematics Education, 14,* 17–47.

Vance, E. (2015). *Class meetings: Young children solving problems together.* Rev. ed. NAEYC.

Van Meeteren, B. (Ed.). (2022a). *Investigating light & shadow with young children.* Teachers College Press.

Van Meeteren, B. (Ed.). (2022b). *Investigating ramps & pathways with young children.* Teachers College Press.

Van Meeteren, B., & Peterson, S. (Eds.). (2022). *Investigating STEM with infants & toddlers.* Teachers College Press.

Verschaffel, L., Greer, B., & De Corte, E. (2007). Whole number concepts and operations. In F. K. Lester (Ed.), *Second handbook of research on mathematics teaching and learning: A project of the National Council of Teachers of Mathematics* (pp. 557–628). Information Age Publishing.

Viterbori, P., Usai, M. C., Traverso, L., & De Franchis, V. (2015). How preschool executive functioning predicts several aspects of math achievement in Grades 1 and 3: A longitudinal study. *Journal of Experimental Child Psychology, 140,* 38–55. http://dx.doi.org/10.1016/j.jecp.2015.06.014

Vitiello, V. E., Greenfield, D. B., Munis, P., & George, J. L. (2011). Cognitive flexibility, approaches to learning, and academic school readiness in head start preschool children. *Early Education & Development, 22*(3), 388–410.

Walker, A. A. (2017). Why education practitioners and stakeholders should care about person fit in educational assessments. *Harvard Educational Review, 87*(3), 426–444.

Walker, C. M., Bonawitz, E., & Lombrozo, T. (2017). Effects of explaining on children's preference for simpler hypotheses. *Psychonomic Bulletin & Review, 24,* 1538–1547. https://doi.org/10.3758/s13423-016-1144-0

Wandersee, J. H. (1990). Concept mapping and the cartography of cognition. *Journal of Research in Science Teaching, 27*(10), 923–936.

Washington, K., Malone, C., Briggs, C., & Reed, G. (2016). Testing African Americans: Testing monograph from the Association of Black Psychologists. In T. L. Leong, & Y. S. Park (Eds.), *Testing and assessment with persons & communities of color* (pp. 1–2). American Psychological Association.

Wildsmith, B. (1987). *All fall down.* Oxford University Press.

Willard, A. K., Busch, J. T., Cullum, K. A., Letourneau, S. M., Sobel, D. M., Callanan, M. A., & Legare, C. H. (2019). Explain this, explore that: A study of parent–child interaction in a children's museum. *Child Development, 90*(5), e598–e617. https://doi.org/10.1111/cdev.13232

Williams, K. M. (2011). Why and how Thinking Maps work: A language of brain and mind. In D. N. Hyerle & L. Alper (Eds.), *Student successes with Thinking Maps.®* 2nd edition (pp. 14–42). Corwin Press.

William and Flora Hewlett Foundation. (2013). Deeper learning competencies. www.hewlett.org/uploads /documents/Deeper_Learning_Defined__April_2013 .pdf

Wilson, P. H., Sztajin, P., Edgington, C., & Confrey, J. (2014). Teachers use of their mathematical knowledge for teaching in learning a mathematics learning trajectory. *Journal of Mathematics Teacher Education*, *17*(2), 149–175.

Wilson, R. (n.d.). Promoting the development of scientific thinking. *Early Childhood News*. www.earlychildhood news.com/earlychildhood/article_pront.aspx?ArticleId =409

Wright, B., Counsell, S., & Tate, S. L. (2015). We're many members, but one body: Fostering a healthy self-identity and agency in African American boys. *Young Children*, *70*(3), 24–31. https://doi.org/10.2307/ycyoungchildren.70.3.24

Yasar, S., Baker, D., Robinson-Kurpius, S., Krause, S., & Roberts, C. (2006). Development of a survey to assess K–12 teachers' perceptions of engineers and familiarity with teaching design, engineering, and technology. *Journal of Engineering Education*, *95*(3), 205–216.

Yee, E., Jones, M. N., & McRae, K. (2018). Semantic memory. *Stevens' Handbook of Experimental Psychology and Cognitive Neuroscience*, *3*, 1–38.

Zan, B., & Geiken, R. (2010). Ramps and pathways: Developmentally appropriate, intellectually rigorous, and fun physical science. *Young Children*, *65*(1), 12–17.

Zelazo, P. D., Blair, C. B., & Willoughby, M. T. (2016). Executive function: Implications for education (NCER 2017-2000). National Center for Education Research, Institute of Education Sciences, U.S. Department of Education. http://ies.ed.gov

Zucker, T. A., Cabell, S. Q., Justice, L. M., Pentimonti, J. M., & Kaderavek, J. N. (2013). The role of frequent, interactive prekindergarten shared reading in the longitudinal development of language and literacy skills. *Developmental Psychology*, *49*(8), 1425–1439.

Index

Accessibility, 6–7, 69
Accommodations, 69–71
Administration for Children & Families Office of Child
    Care, 87, 88
Airasian, P. W., 74
Akiba, M., 14
Aldemir, J., 47
All Fall Down (Wildsmith), 82
Alper, L., 1, 5
Alvarez, A., 34, 35, 46
American Institutes for Research, 31
Anastasi, A., 73
Annie E. Casey Foundation, xiii
Armbruster, B. B., 91
Assessment and documentation, 72–80
Auditory skill development, 18–20

Baillargeon, R., 25
Ballou, D., 14
Bank Street Approach, 58
Barkman, R. C., 4
Bauer, J. R., 25, 33, 46, 53, 54
Belsky, J., 60
Berk, K., 58
Berliner, D., 73
Bierman, K. L., 28
Bitter, C., 31
Blair, C., 81, 83
Block, M. K., 18, 35
Blömeke, S., 42
Bloom, B. S., 91
Bodovski, K., 6
Bodrova, E., 59
Bonawitz, E., 48, 54
Boody, R. M., 63
Booth, A. E., 25, 33, 34, 35, 46, 48, 51, 53, 54
Bor, D., 4
Bowers, E. P., 18, 24
Boyce, W. T., 28
Boykin, A. W., 63
Brace Maps, 11, 35, 39, 48
Brain, function and plasticity, 4, 31–32, 91;
    See also Cognition and cognitive development

Bredekamp, S., 58
Brenneman, K., 9, 47
Bridge Maps, 35, 38, 39, 41, 53–54, 75
Brooks, J. G., 4
Brown, C., 28, 29
Brown Bear, Brown Bear, What Do You See? (Martin), 82
Bubble Maps, 10, 15, 21, 32, 33, 52, 55
Busch, J. T., 54
Butler, L. P., 51

C3 Framework for Social Studies State Standards, 89
Caine, G., 4, 91
Caine, R. N., 4, 91
Camera, L., 66
Cameron, C. E., 20, 83, 84
Carey, S., 24
Castro, D. C., 67
CDC (Centers for Disease Control and Prevention), 64
Center for American Progress, 72
Center on the Developing Child at Harvard University, 28
Centration, 16, 28
Champagne, F. A., 32
Chappuis, J., 74
Checa, P., 81
Chen, Z., 47
Children's literature and interactive reading, 34–41, 82
Chow, B., 31
Circle Maps, 10, 14–15, 19, 26, 35, 62, 74–76
Civil, M., 67
Claessens, A., 25, 42
Clarke, J. H., 91, 92
Classification activities, 14, 84; *See also* Tree Maps
Class meetings, 64–65
Classroom assessments, 74–80
Clements, D. H., 9, 25, 44
Cognition and cognitive development, 11, 12, 24–28,
    70, 83–84; *See also* Executive function skills; Brain,
    function and plasticity
Color-coded maps, 16
Colunga, E., 32
Combita, L. M., 81
Common Core State Standards, 73, 89
Conceptual mapping, 2, 91

Concreteness, 25–26, 91
Conflict resolution, 65–66
Connor, C. M., 67
Constructivist theory, 4, 52, 58, 63, 65, 81
Cooper, D. H., 34
Cooperation and collaboration, 63–66, 84–85
Copley, J. V., 58
Costa, Arthur, 7, 85, 87
Council of Chief State School Officers, 72
Counsell, Shelly, 3, 6, 9, 20, 31, 32, 44, 48, 51, 52, 54, 63,
    72, 73
COVID-19 pandemic, xiii
Creative Curriculum, 58–59
Cultural deprivation model, 72–73
Culturally Different Model, 73–74
Cunha, F., 29
Curran, F. C., 25
Curtis, S., 1

Danko-McGhee, K., 47
Darling-Hammond, L., 14, 72
De Deyne, S., 4
De Franchis, V., 82
DeLoache, J. S., 35
Democratic learning, 60–71
Denham, S. A., 28, 29
Department of Health & Human Services, 28
Developmental Interaction Approach, 58
Developmentally Appropriate Practice (DAP), 22–24
Developmental Studies Center (DSC), 64
DeVries, R., 3, 52, 54, 63, 65, 66
Dewey, John, 58
Diamond, A., 28, 82, 83
Diamond, K. E., 81
Dickinson, D. K., 18, 32, 34
Differentiated instruction, 69–71
Disabilities, 67–68
Diversity and inclusion considerations, 6–7, 66–68
Division of Early Childhood (DEC), 69
Documentation and assessment, 72–80
Dodge, D. T., 58
Doebel, S., 24
Does Deeper Learning Improve Student Outcomes, 31
Double-Bubble Maps, 3, 13, 27, 40, 48–49, 53, 84
Dual Language Learners (DLLs), 67
Duke, N. K., 18, 35
Duncan, J., 4

Early Learning Guidelines (ELGs), 87–88
Ehlert, Lois, 38
Elementary standards, 89
Elia, I., 11
Elstgeest, J., 51
Empathetic understanding, 86
Engel, M., 14, 25, 42

Engineering design, 54–55
Environmental awareness, 49–52
Epigenetics, 24, 28, 32
Epstein, A. S., 58
Esteban-Guitart, M., 67
Everyone Poops (Gomi), 10, 19
Executive function skills, 81–84, 88
Exploring the Intersection of Science Education and
    21st Century Skills, 44
Expressive language, 16, 18, 34–35

Fagiolini, M., 32
Farkas, G., 6
Farrant, B. M., 34
Feuerstein, Reuven, xiv
Fine and gross motor considerations, 70–71
Finegood, E. D., 24
Flora Hewlett Foundation, 31
Flow Maps, 11, 12–13, 39, 41–42, 44, 55, 65–66,
    82–83
Ford, D. Y., 66
Fox, S. E., 28, 31
Frames of reference, 15, 16–18, 19, 75, 91
French, L., 10
Froebel, Friedrich, 20
Froggy Gets Dressed (London), 82

Gage, N. L., 91
Gallets, M., 34
Gámez, P. B., 18, 24
Gamire, E., 55
Gardner, H., 82
Garner, A. S., 28
Gatewood, S., 51
Geiken, R., 52
Gelman, S. A., 47
General learning competencies, 29–30
Gerde, H. K., 47
Glass, G., 73
Goldilocks and the Three Bears, 35–38, 89
Goleman, D., 3, 91, 92
Gomi, Taro, 10
Gonzales, P., 47
Gopnik, A., 24, 46
Grantham, T. C., 66
Graphic organizers, 2–3, 91
Graphic primitives, 11, 12
Gray, S., 82
Greenfield, D. B., 47
Greenwood, C., 18, 24
Greif, M. L., 34, 35, 46
Griebling, S., 57
Griffiths, T. L., 4
Grissmer, D. K., 29
Grissom, J. A., 66

Gross motor considerations, 70–71
Grouws, D. A., 9

Habits of mind, 85–87
Haden, C. A., 48, 51, 53, 54
Hall, D. G., 34
Hamre, B. K., 61
Harris, P. L., 24
Head Start Early Learning Outcomes Framework, 88
Health and physical development, 29
Healy, S. D., 4
Heckman, J. J., 28, 29
Helm, J. H., 15, 57
Henrichs, L. F., 47
Hensch, T. K., 31
Heroman, C., 58
Hiebert, J. C., 9
High/Scope Curriculum, 58
Holland, A. C., 4
Huang, Y. T., 34
Hurly, T. A., 4
Hyerle, David, 1–2, 3, 4, 5, 6, 12, 16, 17, 18, 19, 24, 25, 28, 63, 65, 69, 74, 81, 85, 86, 87, 91, 92

If You Give a Mouse a Cookie (Numeroff), 82
Inclusion, 66–68
Inferiority/pathology model, 72–73
Influencing Frames, 17
Inhibitory control, 84
Inquiry Teaching Model (ITM), 44–46, 74
Institute of Medicine (IOM), 22, 24, 81
IOM & NRC (Institute of Medicine and National Research Council), 11, 14, 22, 23, 25, 28, 32, 34, 35
Iowa Regents' Center for Early Developmental Education (IRCEDE), 44
Isaacs, J. B., 18, 24
Isenberg, J. P., 57

Jackson, Yvette, 6, 22, 32, 60
Jacobs, K., 51
Jacoby, J. W., 25
Jalongo, M. R., 57
Jensen, C. L., 32
Jirout, J., 51
Johnson, James, 57
Jones, C., 58
Jones, M. N., 4

Kallick, B., 7, 85
Kamii, C., 66
Katz, L. G., 15, 57
Keats, Ezra Jack, 40
Kelemen, D., 34, 47
Kelly, K., 16

Kensinger, E. A., 4
Kermani, H., 47
Kieffer, M. J., 18, 32
Kim, H., 21
Kipping, P., 18, 32
Klahr, D., 47
Kliewer, C., 65
Knowledge
    and constructivism, 4
    content knowledge, 10–11, 18, 79–80
    definition and overview, 9, 91
    knowledge construction, 25, 81
    prior knowledge, 14–15, 79–80
    and visual tools, 2
Kobor, M. S., 28
Koenig, M. A., 24
Kohn, A., 20, 58, 63
Kotaman, H., 47
Kuhn, D., 44
Kurzweil, R., 4
K-W-L approach (Know, Want-to-know, Learned), 14–15, 35

Lam, L. L., 24
Language, Thinking Maps as, 11–12
Language skills, 18–20, 32–41, 70
Lavin, T. S., 34
Learning trajectories, 9–12
Lee, J. S., 34
Legare, C. H., 48, 54
Leong, T. L., 59, 73
Lesaux, N. K., 18, 25, 32
Levin, J. R., 33
Levine, S. C., 18, 24
Levitt, P., 28
Lewin-Benham, A., 57
Lindsay, G. W., 4
Ling, D. S., 82, 83
Literacy, 34–41, 82
Llopart, M., 67
Logical-mathematical reasoning, 42–44
Lombrozo, T., 48
London, Jonathan, 82
Loney, E., 31
Lyman, F. T., Jr., 91

Manipulative learning tools, 20–21
Mantzicopoulos, P., 46
Maps and mapping, 2–3, 91
Marcis, D. M., 48
Marriott, S., 35
Martens, M. L., 51
Martin, Bill, Jr., 82
Marzano, R. J., 4
Mashburn, A. J., 32

Mathematics and logical-mathematical reasoning, 42–44
Mattson, M. P., 4
McClelland, M. M., 81
McGroarty-Torres, K., 25, 33
McRae, K., 4
McTighe, J., 91
McWilliams, M. S., 41
Meaney, M. J., 28
Meltzer, L., 81, 82
Memory, working, 82–83
Mental models, 91
Messier, S., 29
Metacognition and metacognitive frames, 16–18, 25–26, 86–87, 91
Meyer, A., 69
Mills, C. M., 51
Modifications and accommodations, 69–71
Montessori, Maria, 20
Moran, S., 82
Motivation, 61–63
Motor skills, 70–71
Multi-Flow Maps, 19–20, 34, 38–39, 65–66

Nagy, W., 18, 32
National Association for the Education of Young Children (NAEYC), 18, 22
National Mathematics Advisory Panel, 10
National Research Council (NRC), 44, 51
National Urban Alliance for Effective Education, 6
Nayfield, L., 47
Nazzi, T., 46
Nelson, C. A., 28
Next Generation Science Standards, 89
NICHD Early Child Care Research Network, 35, 64
Nichols, S., 73
Numeroff, Laura, 82

O'Connor, R. E., 14, 32, 34, 67
Office of Child Care, 87, 88
Office of Special Education, 66
Olmedo, E. L., 66

Pagani, L., 29
Palmer, M., 48
Park, Y. S., 73
Patrick, H., 46
Pattern detection, 4, 24, 91
Pattern Language, Thinking Maps as, 11–12
Patterns of thinking, 91
Pearson, G., 55
Peat, F., 20, 48
Performance-based assessments, 74
Perkins, S. C., 24
Permanent products for assessment, 75–80

Perry Preschool Project, 58
Peterson, S. M., 10, 44
Phillips, S., 16
Physical science, 52–54
Piaget, Jean, 3, 11, 14, 15, 20, 46, 65, 67, 81, 85, 92
Pianta, R. C., 64
Pickering, D. J., 4
Pinto, R., 28
Pittenger, L., 72
Plank, D. N., 72
Plasticity, brain, 31–32
Pollock, J. E., 4
Porche, M. V., 18, 32, 34
Portfolios, 75
Problem-based learning, 58
Process learning, 86–87, 91–92
Proctor, S. L., 68
Project Approach, 15, 57
Put Reading First (Armbruster), 91

Race to the Top Early Learning Challenge (RTT-ELC), 58, 73, 87–88
Ramps and Pathways, 52–53, 54–55
Raudenbush, S. W., 10
Raver, C. C., 81
Reardon, S. F., 63
Receptive language, 16, 18, 34–35
Redding, C., 66
Reese, E., 47
Reese, W. J., 72
Reflective Frames, 17, 86
Reggio Emilia approach, 57–58
Reynolds, C. R., 66, 73
Rhodes, S. M., 82
Robertson, S.-J. L., 47
Robinson-Cimpian, J. P., 63
Roopnarine, Jaipaul, 57
Rose, D. H., 69
Rudd, L. C., 42
Rudick, S., 58
Rueda, M. R., 81
Rugg, M. D., 33
Russell, M. K., 74
Rutter, M., 24, 28

Sackes, M., 47
Sales, C., 3, 52
Samarapungavan, A., 46
Sander, M., 3, 6
Sarama, J., 9, 10, 25, 44
Savelyev, P., 28
Saxe, R., 25
Scaffolding learning, 9, 10, 21, 46, 60, 68–69
Schemas, 3–4, 81, 92

Schulz, L. E., 46
Schunn, C., 4
Schwarz, C. V., 51
Schweinhart, L. J., 58
Scientific thinking, 44–54, 84
Selden, S., 72
Self-regulation, 84–85
Semantic maps, 92
Sénéchal, M., 34
Shavlik, M., 25, 46, 48, 49, 51, 53, 54
Shonkoff, J. P., 28
Show and Tell, 32–34
Siegel, D. J., 65
Singham, M., 72
Slutsky, R., 47
Smith, L. B., 32, 33
Smithsonian Science Education Center, 20
Snider, K. A., 15
Snowballs (Ehlert), 38–41
The Snowy Day (Keats), 40–41
Sobel, D. M., 48
Social studies instruction, 55–57
Socio-economic status (SES) of children, xiii, 63
Socioemotional development, 28–29, 71
Source Frames, 17
Standardized testing, 72–74
Standards, learning, 87–89
Standards Movement, 73
STEM Learning with Young Children (Counsell), 44
Steyvers, M., 4
Stipek, D., 63
Storms, G., 4
Storybook reading, interactive, 34–41, 82
Student Successes with Thinking Maps (Hyerle), 12
Stuhlman, M. W., 64
Styles, D., 64
Suggate, S., 35
Swain, J. E., 24
Swanson, H. L., 82
Systems diagramming and thinking, 2, 92

Tactile materials, 20–21
Takesian, A. E., 31
Tao, Y., 47
Tate, S. L., 32
Technology and engineering design, 54–55
Tekin, A. K., 47
Tenenbaum, J. B., 4
Thelen, E., 21
Thinking Maps
  critical attributes of, 12–14
  definition and overview, 1–3, 92
  early childhood use, 3–4
  as educational framework, 4–7

prior knowledge and experience, 14–15
  in settings outside school, 5–6
Thinking Maps: A Language for Learning (Hyerle & Yeager),
  18, 87
Thompson, R. A., 25, 64
Tools of the Mind, 59
Townsend, D., 18, 32
Trafton, A., 4
Traverso, L., 82
Tree Maps, 1, 11, 13, 28, 36, 42, 53, 65, 75, 84
Trilling, B., 31

Uhlenberg, J., 52
Uncapher, M. R., 33
Universally Designed Learning (UDL), 15–21, 68, 69
Upton, A., 1
Urbina, S., 73
Usai, M. C., 82

VAKT Approach (learning modalities), 15, 21
Valentino, R. A., 63
Vance, E., 64
van den Heuvel-Panhuizen, M., 11
van Ijzendoorn, M. H., 60
Van Meeteren, B., 44, 52, 54
Vasilyeva, M., 18, 24
Venn Diagrams, 84
Verschaffel, L., 9
Visual tools, 2, 92
Visual Tools for Constructing Knowledge (Hyerle), 2
Visual Tools for Transforming Information Into Knowledge
  (Hyerle), 2
Viterbori, P., 82
Vitiello, V. E., 29
Vocabulary acquisition and development, 16, 18, 24–25,
  34–35, 67
Vygotsky, Lev, 35, 59, 68

Walker, A. A., 72, 73
Walker, C. M., 48
Wandersee, J. H., 4
Washington, K., 73
Waxman, S. R., 34
Weathers, E. S., 63
Weikart, David, 58
Wellman, H. M., 24
"Wheels on the Bus" (song), 41
Wildsmith, Brian, 82
Wilhoit, G., 72
Willard, A. K., 48, 54
Williams, K. M., 63, 74
Willoughby, M. T., 81, 83
Wilson, P. H., 9, 10
Wilson, T., 60

Working memory, 82–83
Wright, B., 32

Yasar, S., 4
Yeager, C., 16, 18, 19, 87
Yee, E., 4
Yoshida, H., 32

Zan, B., 3, 52, 54, 63, 65
Zelazo, P. D., 81, 83
Zimmerman, C., 51
Zone of proximal development (ZPD),
        68–69
Zubrick, S. R., 34
Zucker, T. A., 34

About the Authors

Shelly L. Counsell is a retired associate professor of early childhood education, an *Early Years* Columnist with NSTA's journal, *Science and Children*, and an early STEM consultant. Her research includes early STEM, inclusion, democratic learning communities, high-stakes testing, and reflective practice. Other titles she has co-authored with Teachers College Press include *STEM Learning with Young Children: Inquiry Teaching With Ramps and Pathways* and *The Brilliance of Black Boys: Cultivating School Success in the Early Grades*. She is also a contributing author on the new guide *Investigating Ramps and Pathways With Young Children* and other titles in the STEM for Our Youngest Learners Series.

David Hyerle is an international leader in the field of thinking process development through teaching, learning, and leading for equity in education. He is the creator of the *Thinking Maps®* language and author of professional development resources published by *Thinking Maps®, Inc.* David is CEO of *Thinking Schools International*, focused on system-wide integrated pre-K–12 approaches using multiple pathways for facilitating thinking. His engaging workshops and keynote presentations are well known, and his bestselling books include *Visual Tools for Transforming Information into Knowledge* (3rd ed.), *Student Successes with Thinking Maps®* (2nd ed.), and *Thinking Friends*, focused on animating fundamental thinking processes with young children.